Vivid

A Knit Shawl Collection

by Knit Picks

Photography by John Cranford
Graphic Design by Lee Meredith

Printed in the United States of America
First Printing, 2020

ISBN 978-1-62767-301-3

Versa Press, Inc.
800-447-7829
www.versapress.com

CONTENTS

DANCE WITH ROSES

by Aud Bergo

FINISHED MEASUREMENTS
74" width at widest point × 16" depth

YARN
Stroll™ (fingering weight, 75% Fine Superwash Merino Wool, 25% Nylon; 231 yards/ 50g): MC Paisley Heather 28187, 2 skeins; CC Sashay Hand Painted 28271, 1 hank

NEEDLES
US 2 (3mm) 24–32" circular needles, or size to obtain gauge
US 3 (3.25mm) 24–32" circular needles, or size to obtain gauge

NOTIONS
Yarn Needle
Cable Needle
Blocking Pins and/or Wires

GAUGE
30 sts and 46 rows = 4" in Garter Stitch on smaller needles, blocked
31 sts and 40 rows = 4" in Rib and Garter Stitch Pattern on smaller needles, blocked
31 sts and 40 rows = 4" in Rib and Purl Stitch Pattern on smaller needles, blocked
31 sts and 40 rows = 4" in Cable Rose Stitch Pattern on larger needles, blocked (gauge is not crucial, but it will affect finished size and yardage requirements)

For pattern support, contact audbergo@hotmail.com

Dance with Roses

Notes:

What better way to celebrate the warmer seasons than with a cabled roses shawl in lovely colors? This sweet accessory can also be saved for cooler times to wrap around the neck more snugly with roses on display.

Dance with Roses is an asymmetrical triangle shawl, worked flat beginning from the narrow end. The 20-stitch wide, 24-row long cable rose pattern is worked in a solid color and separated with Garter Stitch and Rib sections. The pattern yields a shawl that is easily blocked into shape to show off the cable roses.

Charts are worked flat; read RS rows (odd numbers) from right to left, and WS rows (even numbers) from left to right.

The pattern is divided into 19 Sections. Each Section can be worked from the chart or from the written description. Each chart is labelled A, B, C etc. and includes the name of the stitch pattern and the section in which it is used.

The shawl is shaped by increase and decrease stitches on every RS row. Knit the last stitch on every RS row loosely for easily blocking later.

The pattern will give instructions for when to break the yarn. Otherwise, carry the unused color under the color just used along the edge.

2/2 LC (cable 2 over 2 left)
Sl2 to CN, hold in front; K2, K2 from CN.

2/2 RC (cable 2 over 2 right)
Sl2 to CN, hold in back; K2, K2 from CN.

2/2 LPC (cable 2 over 2 left, purl back)
Sl2 to CN, hold in front; P2, K2 from CN.

2/2 RPC (cable 2 over 2 right, purl back)
Sl2 to CN, hold in back; K2, P2 from CN.

2/2/2 LPC (cable 2 over 2 left, purl 2 center back)
Sl4 to CN, hold in front; K2, Sl 2 leftmost sts from CN to LH needle, P these 2, K2 from CN.

KFBF (knit front back front)
Knit into front and back of stitch and again into front to inc from 1 st to 3 sts.

Rib and Garter Pattern (flat over 10 sts)
Row 1 (RS): K across.
Row 2 (WS): K8, P2.
Rep Rows 1–2 for pattern.

Rib and Purl Pattern (flat over 10 sts)
Row 1 (RS): K2, P8.
Row 2 (WS): K8, P2.
Rep Rows 1–2 for pattern.

Cable Rose Pattern (flat over 20 sts)
Row 1 (RS): K2, P18.
Row 2 (WS): K2, P2, K10, P2, K2, P2.
Row 3: K2, P2, 2/2 LC, P6, 2/2 RC, P2.
Row 4: K2, P4, K6, P4, K2, P2.
Row 5: K2, P2, K2, 2/2 LPC, P2, 2/2 RPC, K2, P2.
Rows 6–8: (K2, P2) five times.
Row 9: K2, P2, 2/2 LPC, K2, P2, K2, 2/2 RPC, P2.
Row 10: K4, P4, K2, P4, K4, P2.
Row 11: K2, P4, 2/2 LPC, P2, 2/2 RPC, K4.
Row 12: K6, P2, K2, P2, K6, P2.
Row 13: K2, P6, 2/2/2 LPC, P6.
Row 14: Rep Row 12.
Row 15: K2, P4, 2/2 RC, P2, 2/2 LC, P4.
Row 16: Rep Row 10.
Row 17: K2, P2, 2/2 RPC, K2, P2, K2, 2/2 LPC, P2.
Rows 18–20: Rep Rows 6–8.
Row 21: K2, P2, K2, 2/2 RPC, P2, 2/2 LPC, K2, P2.
Row 22: K2, P4, K6, P4, K2, P2.
Row 23: K2, P2, 2/2 RPC, P6, 2/2 LPC, P2.
Row 24: K18, P2.

DIRECTIONS

Setup
With CC and smaller needles, CO 5 sts.
Row 1 (RS): K1, K2tog, KFBF, K1. 6 sts.
Row 2 (WS): K across.

Section 1: Garter Stitch Pattern
Row 1 (RS): K1, K2tog, K to last 2 sts, KFBF, K1. 1 st inc.
Row 2 (WS): K across.
Rep Rows 1–2 until there are 70 sts, ending with a RS Row.
Next Row (WS): (K8, P2) six times, K10.

Section 2: Rib and Purl Stitch Pattern
Join MC and work Chart A or as follows.
Row 1 (RS): K1, K2tog, P7, work Rib and Purl Pattern Row 1 five times, K2, P6, KFBF, K1. 71 sts.
Row 2 (WS): K10, P2, work Rib and Purl Pattern Row 2 five times, K9.
Row 3: K1, K2tog, P6, work Rib and Purl Pattern Row 1 six times, KFBF, K1. 72 sts.
Row 4: K2, P2, work Rib and Purl Stitch Pattern Row 2 six times, K8.
Row 5: K1, K2tog, P5, work Rib and Purl Pattern Row 1 six times, K2, KFBF, K1. 73 sts.
Row 6: K4, P2, work Rib and Purl Pattern Row 2 six times, K7.

Section 3: Rib and Garter Stitch Pattern
With CC, work Chart B or as follows.
Row 1 and all RS rows: K1, K2tog, K to last 2 sts, KFBF, K1. 1 st inc.
Row 2 (WS): K6, P2, work Rib and Garter Pattern Row 2 six times, K6.
Row 4: Work Rib and Garter Pattern Row 2 seven times, K5.

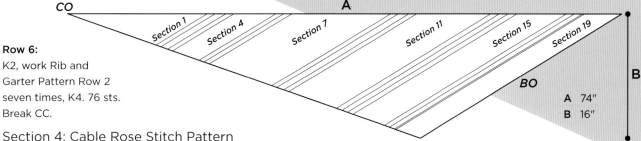

Row 6:
K2, work Rib and Garter Pattern Row 2 seven times, K4. 76 sts. Break CC.

Section 4: Cable Rose Stitch Pattern
Change to larger needles and MC.
Work Chart C or as follows.
Row 1 (RS): K1, K2tog, P1, K2, P8, work Cable Rose Pattern Row 1 three times, KFBF, K1. 77 sts.
Row 2 (WS): K2, P2, work Cable Rose Pattern Row 2 three times, K8, P2, K3.
Row 3): K1, K2tog, K2, P8, work Cable Rose Pattern Row 3 three times, K2, KFBF, K1. 78 sts.
Row 4: K4, P2, work Cable Rose Pattern Row 4 three times, K8, P2, K2.
Row 5: K1, K2tog, K1, P8, work Cable Rose Pattern Row 5 three times, K2, P2, KFBF, K1. 79 sts.
Row 6: K6, P2, work Cable Rose Pattern Row 6 three times, K8, P1, K2.
Row 7: K1, K2tog, P8, work Cable Rose Pattern Row 7 three times, K2, P4, KFBF, K1. 80 sts.
Row 8: K8, P2, work Cable Rose Pattern Row 8 three times, K10.
Row 9: K1, K2tog, P7, work Cable Rose Pattern Row 9 three times, K2, P6, KFBF, K1. 81 sts.
Row 10: K10, P2, work Cable Rose Pattern Row 10 three times, K9.
Row 11: K1, K2tog, P6, work Cable Rose Pattern Row 11 three times, K2, P8, KFBF, K1. 82 sts.
Row 12: K2, P2, K8, P2, work Cable Rose Pattern Row 12 three times, K8.
Row 13: K1, K2tog, P5, work Cable Rose Pattern Row 13 three times, K2, P8, K2, KFBF, K1. 83 sts.
Row 14: K4, P2, K8, P2, work Cable Rose Pattern Row 14 three times, K7.
Row 15: K1, K2tog, P4, work Cable Rose Pattern Row 15 three times, K2, P8, K2, P2, KFBF, K1. 84 sts.
Row 16: K6, P2, K8, P2, work Cable Rose Pattern Row 16 three times, K6.
Row 17: K1, K2tog, P3, work Cable Rose Pattern Row 17 three times, K2, P8, K2, P4, KFBF, K1. 85 sts.
Row 18: (K8, P2) two times, work Cable Rose Pattern Row 18 three times, K5.
Row 19: K1, K2tog, P2, work Cable Rose Pattern Row 19 three times, K2, P8, K2, P6, KFBF, K1. 86 sts.
Row 20: K10, P2, K8, P2, work Cable Rose Pattern Row 20 three times, K4.
Row 21: K1, K2tog, P1, work Cable Rose Pattern Row 21 three times, (K2, P8) two times, KFBF, K1. 87 sts.
Row 22: K2, P2, (K8, P2) two times, work Cable Rose Pattern Row 22 three times, K3.
Row 23: K1, K2tog, work Cable Rose Pattern Row 23 three times, (K2, P8) two times, K2, KFBF, K1. 88 sts.

Row 24: K4, P2, (K8, P2) two times, work Cable Rose Pattern Row 24 three times, K2.

Section 5: Rib and Garter Stitch Pattern
Change to smaller needles and join CC. Work Chart D or as follows.
Row 1 and all RS rows: K1, K2tog, K to last 2 sts, KFBF, K1. 1 st inc.
Row 2 (WS): K6, P2, work Rib and Garter Pattern Row 2 seven times, K11.
Row 4: Work Rib and Garter Pattern Row 2 eight times, K10.
Row 6: K2, work Rib and Garter Pattern Row 2 eight times, K9. 91 sts.

Section 6: Rib and Purl Stitch Pattern
With MC, work Chart E or as follows.
Row 1 (RS): K1, K2tog, P6, work Rib and Purl Pattern Row 1 eight times, KFBF, K1. 92 sts.
Row 2 (WS): K2, P2, work Rib and Purl Pattern Row 2 eight times, K8.
Row 3: K1, K2tog, P5, work Rib and Purl Pattern Row 1 eight times, K2, KFBF, K1. 93 sts.
Row 4: K4, P2, work Rib and Purl Pattern Row 2 eight times, K7.
Row 5: K1, K2tog, P4, work Rib and Purl Pattern Row 1 eight times, K2, P2, KFBF, K1. 94 sts.
Row 6: K6, P2, work Rib and Purl Pattern Row 2 eight times, K6.
Break MC.

Section 7: Garter Stitch Pattern
With CC work as follows.
Row 1 (RS): K1, K2tog, K to last 2 sts, KFBF, K1. 1 st inc.
Row 2 (WS): K across.
Rep Rows 1–2 until there are 130 sts, ending with a RS Row.
Next Row (WS): (K8, P2) twelve times, K10.

Section 8: Rib and Purl Stitch Pattern
Join MC and work Chart A or follow written instructions for Section 2—for this section, Rib and Purl Pattern is worked six more times across, a total of eleven and twelve times. 133 sts.

Section 9: Rib and Garter Stitch Pattern
With CC, work Chart B or follow written instructions for Section 3—for this section, Rib and Garter Pattern is worked six more times across, a total of twelve and thirteen times. 136 sts.
Break CC.

Section 10: Cable Rose Stitch Pattern

Change to larger needles and MC.

Work Chart C or follow written instructions for Section 4—for this section, Cable Rose Pattern is worked three more times across, a total of six times. 148 sts.

Section 11: Cable Rose Stitch Pattern

Section 11 adds a second Cable Rose Pattern to previous Section. With MC, work Chart F or as follows.

Row 1 (RS): K1, K2tog, K1, P8, K2, P8, work Cable Rose Pattern Row 1 six times, K2, P2, KFBF, K1. 149 sts.

Row 2 (WS): K6, P2, work Cable Rose Pattern Row 2 six times, K8, P2, K8, P1, K2.

Row 3: K1, K2tog, P8, K2, P8, work Cable Rose Pattern Row 3 six times, K2, P4, KFBF, K1. 150 sts.

Row 4: K8, P2, work Cable Rose Pattern Row 4 six times, K8, P2, K10.

Row 5: K1, K2tog, P7, K2, P8, work Cable Rose Pattern Row 5 six times, K2, P6, KFBF, K1. 151 sts.

Row 6: K10, P2, work Cable Rose Pattern Row 6 six times, K8, P2, K9.

Row 7: K1, K2tog, P6, K2, P8, work Cable Rose Pattern Row 7 six times, K2, P8, KFBF, K1. 152 sts.

Row 8: K2, P2, K8, P2, work Cable Rose Pattern Row 8 six times, K8, P2, K8.

Row 9: K1, K2tog, P5, K2, P8, work Cable Rose Pattern Row 9 six times, K2, P8, K2, KFBF, K1. 153 sts.

Row 10: K4, P2, K8, P2, work Cable Rose Pattern Row 10 six times, K8, P2, K7.

Row 11: K1, K2tog, P4, K2, P8, work Cable Rose Pattern Row 11 six times, K2, P8, K2, P2, KFBF, K1. 154 sts.

Row 12: K6, P2, K8, P2, work Cable Rose Pattern Row 12 six times, K8, P2, K6.

Row 13: K1, K2tog, P3, K2, P8, work Cable Rose Pattern Row 13 six times, K2, P8, K2, P4, KFBF, K1. 155 sts.

Row 14: (K8, P2) two times, work Cable Rose Pattern Row 14 six times, K8, P2, K5.

Row 15: K1, K2tog, P2, K2, P8, work Cable Rose Pattern Row 15 six times, K2, P8, K2, P6, KFBF, K1. 156 sts.

Row 16: K2, (K8, P2) two times, work Cable Rose Pattern Row 16 six times, K8, P2, K4.

Row 17: K1, K2tog, P1, K2, P8, work Cable Rose Pattern Row 17 six times, (K2, P8) two times, KFBF, K1. 157 sts.

Row 18: K2, P2, (K8, P2) two times, work Cable Rose Pattern Row 18 six times, K8, P2, K3.

Row 19: K1, K2tog, K2, P8, work Cable Rose Pattern Row 19 six times, (K2, P8) two times, K2, KFBF, K1. 158 sts.

Row 20: K4, P2, (K8, P2) two times, work Cable Rose Pattern Row 20 six times, K8, P2, K2.

Row 21: K1, K2tog, K1, P8, work Cable Rose Pattern Row 21 six times, (K2, P8) two times, K2, P2, KFBF, K1. 159 sts.

Row 22: K6, P2, (K8, P2) two times, work Cable Rose Pattern Row 22 six times, K8, P1, K2.

Row 23: K1, K2tog, K8, work Cable Rose Pattern Row 23 six times, (K2, P8) two times, K2, P4, KFBF, K1. 160 sts.

Row 24: (K8, P2) three times, work Cable Rose Pattern Row 24 six times, K10.

Section 12: Rib and Garter Stitch Pattern

Change to smaller needles and join CC. Work Chart G or as follows.

Row 1 and all RS rows: K1, K2tog, K to two last sts, KFBF, K1. 1 st inc.

Row 2 (WS): K10, P2, work Rib and Garter Pattern Row 2 fourteen times, K9.

Row 4: K2, P2, work Rib and Garter Pattern Row 2 fifteen times, K8.

Row 6: K4, P2, work Rib and Garter Pattern Row 2 fifteen times, K7. 163 sts.

Section 13: Rib and Purl Stitch Pattern

With MC, work Chart H or as follows.

Row 1 (RS): K1, K2tog, P4, work Rib and Purl Pattern Row 1 fifteen times, K2, P2, KFBF, K1. 164 sts.

Row 2 (WS): K6, P2, work Rib and Purl Pattern Row 2 fifteen times, K6.

Row 3: K1, K2tog, P3, work Rib and Purl Pattern Row 1 fifteen times, K2, P4, KFBF, K1. 165 sts.

Row 4: K8, P2, work Rib and Purl Pattern Row 2 fifteen times, K5.

Row 5: K1, K2tog, P2, work Rib and Purl Pattern Row 1 fifteen times, K2, P6, KFBF, K1. 166 sts

Row 6: K10, P2, Rib and Purl Pattern Row 2 fifteen times, K4.

Section 14: Rib and Garter Stitch Pattern

With CC, work Chart I or as follows.

Row 1 (RS): K1, K2tog, K to last 2 sts, KFBF, K1. 1 st inc.

Row 2 (WS): K2, P2, work Rib and Garter Pattern Row 2 sixteen times, K3.

Row 3: Rep Row 1. 168 sts.

Row 4: K4, P2, work Rib and Garter Pattern Row 2 sixteen times, K2.

Row 5: K across.

Row 6: Rep Row 4.

Break CC.

Section 15: Cable Rose Stitch Pattern

Change to larger needles and MC.

Work Chart F or follow written instructions for Section 11—for this section, Cable Rose pattern is worked one more time across, a total of seven times. 180 sts.

Section 16: Rib and Garter Stitch Pattern

Change to smaller needles and join CC.

Work Chart G or follow written instructions for Section 12—for this section, Rib and Garter pattern is worked two more times across, a total of sixteen and seventeen times. 183 sts.

Section 17: Rib and Purl Stitch Pattern

With MC, work Chart H or follow written instructions for Section 13—for this section, Rib and Purl pattern is worked two more times across, a total of seventeen times. 186 sts. Break MC.

Section 18: Rib and Garter Stitch Pattern

With CC, work two rows as follows.

Row 1 (RS): K1, K2tog, K to last 2 sts, KFBF, K1. 187 sts.

Row 2 (WS): K2, P2, (K8, P2) 18 times, K3.

Section 19: Garter Stitch Pattern

With CC, work as follows.

Row 1 (RS): K1, K2tog, K to last 2 sts, KFBF, K1. 1 st inc.

Row 2 (WS): K across.

Rep Rows 1–2 until there are 205 sts, ending with a WS Row.

With RS facing, BO all sts P-wise.

Finishing

Weave in ends and block.

LEGEND

No Stitch
Placeholder—no stitch made

K
RS: Knit stitch
WS: Purl stitch

P
RS: Purl stitch
WS: Knit stitch

K2tog
Knit 2 stitches together as one stitch

KFBF
Knit into the front, then the back,
then the front again, o⁻ the stitch

Cable 2 Over 2 Right (2/2 RC)
Sl2 to CN, hold in back; K2, K2 from CN

Cable 2 Over 2 Left (2/2 LC)
Sl2 to CN, hold in front; K2, K2 from CN

Cable 2 Over 2 Right, Purl back (2/2 RPC)
Sl2 to CN, hold in back; K2, P2 from CN

Cable 2 Over 2 Left, Purl back (2/2 LPC)
Sl2 to CN, hold in front; P2, K2 from CN

Cable 2 Over 2 Left, Purl 2 center back (2/2/2 LPC)
Sl4 to CN, hold in front; K2, Sl 2 leftmost sts from CN
to left-hand needle, P these 2, K2 from CN

Pattern Repeat

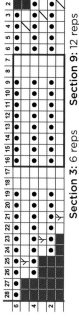

Chart B: Rib and Garter, Sections 3 & 9

Section 3: 6 reps   Section 9: 12 reps

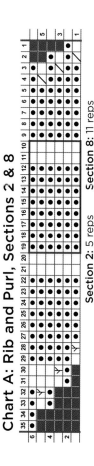

Chart A: Rib and Purl, Sections 2 & 8

Section 2: 5 reps   Section 8: 11 reps

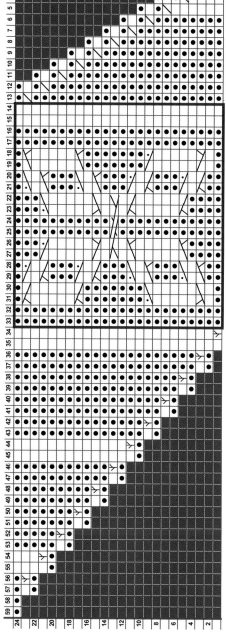

Chart C: Cable Rose, Sections 4 & 10

Section 4: 3 reps   Section 10: 6 reps

Chart E: Rib and Purl, Section 6

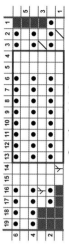

Section 6: 8 reps

Chart D: Rib and Garter, Section 5

Section 5: 7 reps

Chart F: Cable Rose, Sections 11 & 15

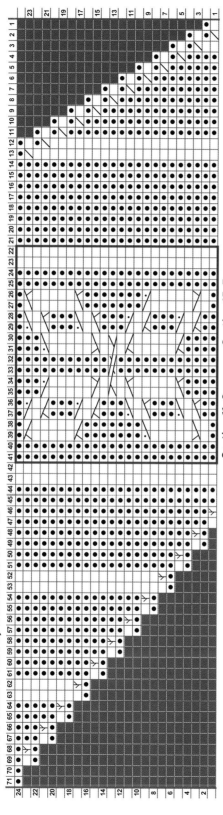

Section 15: 7 reps

Section 11: 6 reps

Chart G: Rib and Garter, Sections 12 & 16

Section 16: 16 reps

Section 12: 14 reps

Chart H: Rib and Purl, Sections 13 & 17

Section 17: 17 reps

Section 13: 15 reps

Chart I: Rib and Garter, Section 14

Section 14: 16 reps

DRAKE'S BEACH

by Stephannie Tallent

FINISHED MEASUREMENTS

103″ width × 49″ depth; 83″ along right bottom edge, 61″ along left bottom edge (this is the top/bind off edge as you knit)

YARN

Capretta™ (fingering weight, 80% Fine Superwash Merino Wool, 10% Cashmere, 10% Nylon; 230 yards/50g): Loganberry 27646, 6 balls

NEEDLES

US 6 (4mm) 24–32″ circular needles, or size to obtain gauge

NOTIONS

Yarn Needle
Stitch Markers
Blocking Pins and/or Wires

GAUGE

14 sts and 16 rows = 4″ in Kelp and Textured patterns, aggressively blocked
16.5 sts and 18 rows = 4″ over Kelp and Textured patterns, relaxed after blocking (this piece is very stretchy while blocking and will relax after unpinning)

For pattern support, contact stephannie@sunsetcat.com

Drake's Beach

Notes:

Pairing a modification of a favorite vintage lace pattern—Print of the Wave—with a pretty dot knit textured design, the patterning mimics kelp strands on a sandy beach.

The Drake's Beach shawl is worked flat as a wedge from side to side with a lace edging along one bottom edge. An optional knitted-on lace bind off is included.

Charts are worked flat; read RS rows (odd numbers) from right to left, and WS rows (even numbers) from left to right, for all charts except the (Optional) Top Edging Setup chart, which begins with a WS row.

The different repeat and increase sections are bordered in different colors.

Use the Swatch Chart to practice the techniques and stitch patterns for this pattern as well as to check gauge.

Size is easily changed by working fewer (or more) repeats. Vigorous blocking will cause the edges to be wider and the length longer than expected by swatch gauge, due to the stretchiness of the yarnover/decrease sections.

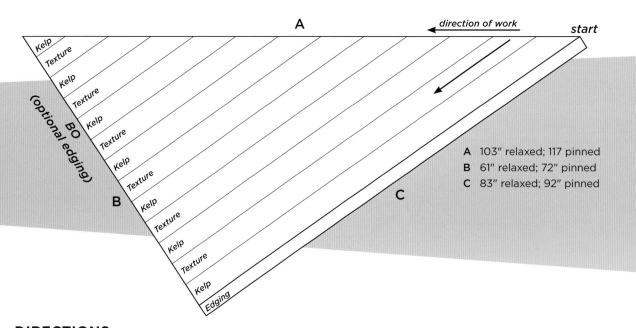

A 103" relaxed; 117" pinned
B 61" relaxed; 72" pinned
C 83" relaxed; 92" pinned

DIRECTIONS

Setup
CO 9 sts.
Work Chart A, PM as indicated, SM as you come to it on subsequent rows.
Work chart Rows 1–66. 40 sts.

Work Chart B, PMs as indicated, SMs as you come to them on subsequent rows.
Work chart Rows 1–72. 76 sts.

Repeats
Textured Increase Row (RS): Work Textured Increase chart, (work Kelp Repeat chart, work Textured Repeat chart) to last Kelp Repeat, work last Kelp Repeat, work Edging Repeat. Cont as established until Rows 1–12 of Textured Increase chart are completed. 6 sts inc; 82 sts.

Kelp Increase Row (RS): Work Kelp Increase, (work Textured Repeat, work Kelp Repeat) to Edging, work Edging Repeat. Cont as established until Kelp Increase chart is completed. 30 sts inc; 112 sts.

Work Textured Increase chart and Kelp Increase chart as established five times total. End the last Kelp Increase chart repeat with Row 59. 259 sts.
Looking at RS of knitting, right to left, there is one complete Kelp Increase section less one row, six sets of Kelp Repeat and Textured Repeat columns, and the Edging Repeat.

BO K-wise or work optional knitted-on lace edging as follows.

Optional Knitted-On Lace Edging
Setup Row (WS): Work Row 1 of Top Edging Setup chart. Complete Top Edging Setup chart.

Work Top Edging chart until all edge sts have been bound off. BO remaining sts K-wise.

Finishing
Weave in ends, wash, and block.

LEGEND

No Stitch
Placeholder—no stitch made

K
RS: Knit stitch
WS: Purl stitch

P
RS: Purl stitch
WS: Knit stitch

K TBL
RS: Knit stitch through the back loop
WS: Purl stitch through the back loop

YO
Yarn over

K2tog
Knit 2 stitches together as one stitch

SSK
Slip, slip, knit slipped stitches together

BO
Bind off 1 stitch

BO st
Stitch remaining on needle after working bind off stitches

CO
Cast on 1 stitch

P2tog (joining edging)
WS: Purl 2 stitches together as one stitch (1 edging stitch together with 1 body stitch)

Edging Repeat

Kelp Repeat

Kelp Increase Wedge

Texture Repeat

Texture Increase Wedge

Swatch Chart

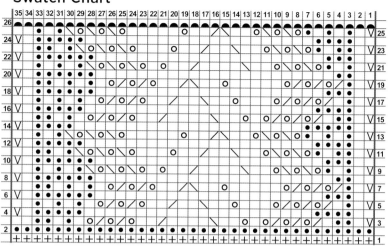

Chart A

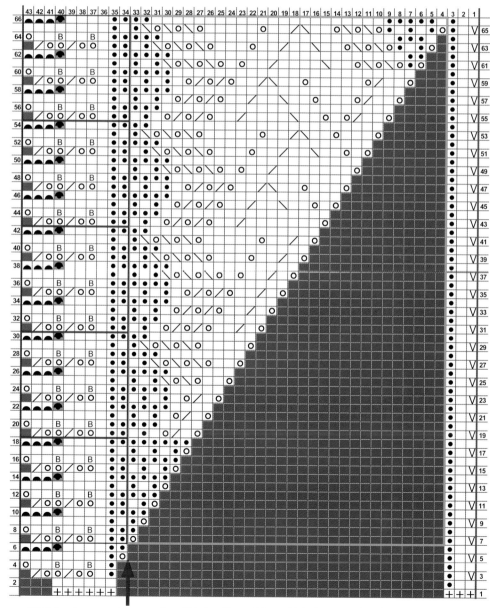

Marker placement, separating Edging Repeat from Kelp Increase Section; once this chart is completed, it will separate Edging Repeat from first Kelp Repeat.

Chart B

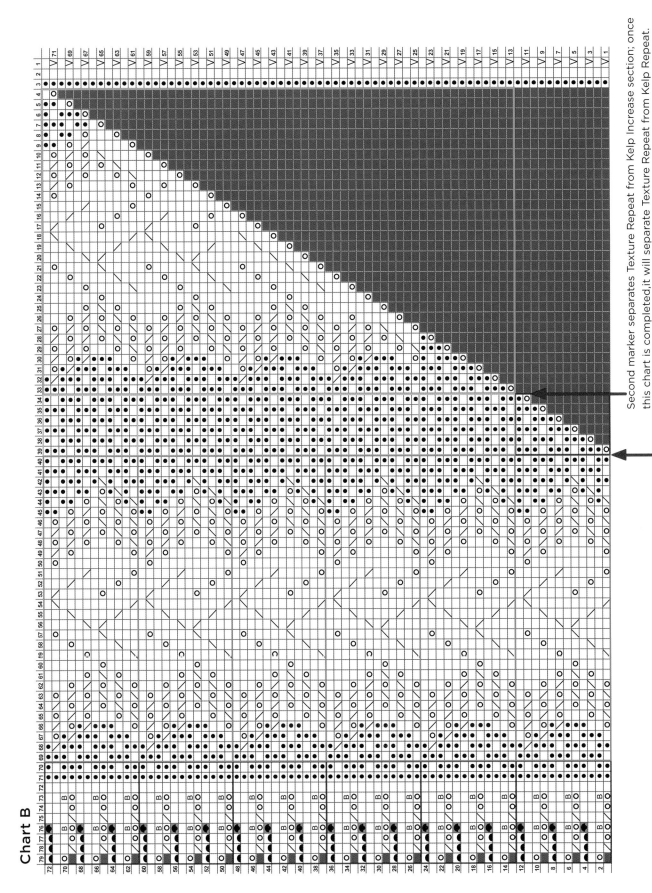

Second marker separates Texture Repeat from Kelp Increase section; once this chart is completed,it will separate Texture Repeat from Kelp Repeat.

First marker separates Kelp Repeat from Texture Increase section; once Row 12 is completed, it will separate Kelp Repeat from Texture Repeat.

Kelp Increase

(Optional) Top Edging

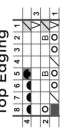

(Optional) Top Edging Setup

Texture Increase

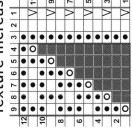

Kelp Repeat

Texture Repeat

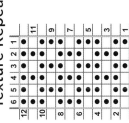
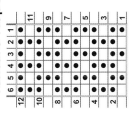
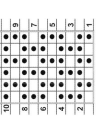

Edging Repeat

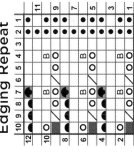

HASHTAG

by Mone Dräger

FINISHED MEASUREMENTS

62″ width at widest point × 32″ depth

YARN

Gloss™ (fingering weight, 70% Merino Wool, 30% Silk; 220 yards/50g): MC Kenai 24612, CC Black 23865, 2 hanks each

NEEDLES

US 2 (3mm) 24–32″ circular needles, or size to obtain gauge

NOTIONS

Yarn Needle
Stitch Markers
Blocking Pins and/or Wires

GAUGE

19 sts and 40 rows = 4″ in Garter Stitch, blocked
19 sts and 40 rows = 4″ in Mosaic Pattern, blocked
(gauge is not crucial, but it will affect finished size and yardage requirements)

For pattern support, contact mone.draeger@web.de

Hashtag

Notes:

The Hashtag shawl combines stripes in Garter Stitch with motifs and borders in mosaic knitting. The mosaic pattern is reminiscent of the hashtag symbol, which has become so popular in the last couple of years.

The shawl is started at one of the top corners and is worked on the bias as a sideways triangle with a centered bottom. It is worked with one color at the time; two rows in MC alternate with two rows in CC. Always pick up the new yarn from under the old yarn for the best looking edge.

Stitch patterns are both written and charted. Only one yarn color is used for each row—on charts, the color of the row number is the color used on that row. Charts are worked flat; read RS rows (odd numbers) from right to left, and WS rows (even numbers) from left to right.

Work all slipped stitches purl-wise with yarn to WS of work (yarn in back on RS rows, yarn in front on WS rows). Optional: Place a locking stitch marker on the RS to more easily keep track of which side is which.

Setup Chart (worked flat)
Stitch counts are in [brackets] for subsequent repeats of the given rows.
Row 1 (RS): With MC, YO, Sl1, K2. 4 sts.
Row 2 (WS): With MC, K2, Sl1, K1 TBL.
Row 3: With CC, YO, K4. 5 sts.
Row 4: With CC, K4, K1 TBL.
Row 5: With MC, YO, (Sl1, K1) two times, K1. 6 sts.
Row 6: With MC, K1, (K1, Sl1) two times, K1 TBL.
Row 7: With CC, YO, (Sl1, K1) three times. 7 sts.
Row 8: With CC, (K1, Sl1) three times, K1 TBL.
Row 9: With MC, YO, K2, Sl1, K4. 8 sts.
Row 10: With MC, K4, Sl1, K2, K1 TBL.
Row 11: With CC, YO, K2, (Sl1, K1) three times. 9 sts.
Row 12: With CC, (K1, Sl1) three times, K2, K1 TBL.
Row 13: With MC, YO, Sl1, K8. 10 sts.
Row 14: With MC, K8, Sl1, K1 TBL.
Row 15: With CC, YO, K6, (Sl1, K1) two times. 11 sts.
Row 16: With CC, (K1, Sl1) two times, K6, K1 TBL.
Row 17: With MC, YO, Sl1, K1, Sl1, K5, Sl1, K2. 12 sts.
Row 18: With MC, K2, Sl1, K5, Sl1, K1, Sl1, K1 TBL.
Row 19: With CC, YO, (Sl1, K1) six times. 13 sts.
Row 20: With CC, (K1, Sl1) six times, K1 TBL.
Row 21: With MC, YO, K2, Sl1, K5, (Sl1, K1) two times, K1. 14 sts.
Row 22: With MC, K2, (Sl1, K1) two times, K4, Sl1, K2, K1 TBL.
Row 23: With CC, YO, (K2, Sl1, K1, Sl1, K7) to last 2 sts, K2. 15 [27, 39] sts.
Row 24: With CC, K2, (K7, Sl1, K1, Sl1, K2) to last st, K1 TBL.
Row 25: With MC, YO, (Sl1, K9, Sl1, K1, Sl1) to last 2 sts, K2. 16 [28, 40] sts.
Row 26: With MC, K2, (Sl1, K1, Sl1, K9) to last 2 sts, Sl1, K1 TBL.
Row 27: With CC, YO, K2, (K4, Sl1, K1, Sl1, K5) to last 2 sts, K2. 17 [29, 41] sts.

Row 28: With CC, K2, (K5, Sl1, K1, Sl1, K4) to last 3 sts, K2, K1 TBL.
Row 29: With MC, YO, Sl1, K1, Sl1, (K5, Sl1, K3, Sl1, K1, Sl1) to last 2 sts, K2. 18 [30, 42] sts.
Row 30: With MC, K2, (Sl1, K1, Sl1, K3, Sl1, K5) to last 4 sts, Sl1, K1, Sl1, K1 TBL.
Row 31: With CC, YO, (Sl1, K1) to end. 19 [31, 43] sts.
Row 32: With CC, (K1, Sl1) to last st, K1 TBL.
Row 33: With MC, YO, K2, Sl1, K2, (K3, Sl1, K1, Sl1, K3, Sl1, K2) to last 2 sts, K2. 20 [32, 44] sts.
Row 34: With MC, K2, (K2, Sl1, K3, Sl1, K1, Sl1, K3) to last 6 sts, K2, Sl1, K2, K1 TBL.
Row 35: With CC, YO, K2, (Sl1, K1) two times, *K8, (Sl1, K1) two times; rep from * to last 2 sts, Sl1, K1. 21 [33, 45] sts.
Row 36: With CC, K1, Sl1, *(K1, Sl1) two times, K8; rep from * to last 7 sts, (K1, Sl1) two times, K2, K1 TBL.
Row 37: With MC, YO, Sl1, K6, (K3, Sl1, K1, Sl1, K6) to last 2 sts, K2. 22 [34] sts.
Row 38: With MC, K2, (K6, Sl1, K1, Sl1, K3) to last 8 sts, K6, Sl1, K1 TBL.
Row 39: With CC, YO, K6, Sl1, K1, (Sl1, K9, Sl1, K1) to last 2 sts, Sl1, K1. 23 [35] sts.
Row 40: With CC, K1, Sl1, (K1, Sl1, K9, Sl1) to last 9 sts, K1, Sl1, K6, K1 TBL.
Row 41: With MC, YO, Sl1, K1, Sl1, K5, Sl1, (K3, Sl1, K1, Sl1, K5, Sl1) to last 2 sts, K2. 24 [36] sts.
Row 42: With MC, K2, (Sl1, K5, Sl1, K1, Sl1, K3) to last 10 sts, Sl1, K5, Sl1, K1, Sl1, K1 TBL.
Row 43: With CC, YO, (Sl1, K1) to end. 25 [37] sts.
Row 44: With CC, (K1, Sl1) to last st, K1 TBL.
Row 45: With MC, YO, K2, Sl1, K5, Sl1, K1, Sl1, (K3, Sl1, K5, Sl1, K1, Sl1) to last 2 sts, K2. 26 [38] sts.
Row 46: With MC, K2, (Sl1, K1, Sl1, K5, Sl1, K3) to last 12 sts, Sl1, K1, Sl1, K5, Sl1, K2, K1 TBL.

Main Chart (flat over a multiple of 12 sts plus 10)
Row 1 (RS): With MC, K8, (K3, Sl1, K1, Sl1, K6) to last 2 sts, K2.
Row 2 (WS): With MC, K2, (K6, Sl1, K1, Sl1, K3) to last 8 sts, K8.
Row 3: With CC, K6, Sl1, K1, (Sl1, K9, Sl1, K1) to last 2 sts, Sl1, K1.
Row 4: With CC, K1, Sl1, (K1, Sl1, K9, Sl1) to last 8 sts, K1, Sl1, K6.
Row 5: With MC, K7, Sl1, (K3, Sl1, K1, Sl1, K5, Sl1) to last 2 sts, K2.
Row 6: With MC, K2, (Sl1, K5, Sl1, K1, Sl1, K3) to last 8 sts, Sl1, K7.
Row 7: With CC, K4, (Sl1, K1) to end.
Row 8: With CC, (K1, Sl1) to last 4 sts, K4.
Row 9: With MC, K5, Sl1, K1, Sl1, (K3, Sl1, K5, Sl1, K1, Sl1) to last 2 sts, K2.
Row 10: With MC, K2, (Sl1, K1, Sl1, K5, Sl1, K3) to last 8 sts, Sl1, K1, Sl1, K5.
Row 11: With CC, Sl1, K7, (K2, Sl1, K1, Sl1, K7) to last 2 sts, K2.
Row 12: With CC, K2, (K7, Sl1, K1, Sl1, K2) to last 8 sts, K7, Sl1.
Row 13: With MC, K5, Sl1, K1, Sl1, (K9, Sl1, K1, Sl1) to last 2 sts, K2.
Row 14: With MC, K2, (Sl1, K1, Sl1, K9) to last 8 sts, Sl1, K1, Sl1, K5.
Row 15: With CC, K2, Sl1, K5, (K4, Sl1, K1, Sl1, K5) to last 2 sts, K2.
Row 16: With CC, K2, (K5, Sl1, K1, Sl1, K4) to last 8 sts, K5, Sl1, K2.

Row 17: With MC, K5, Sl1, K1, Sl1, (K5, Sl1, K3, Sl1, K1, Sl1) to last 2 sts, K2.
Row 18: With MC, K2, (Sl1, K1, Sl1, K3, Sl1, K5) to last 8 sts, Sl1, K1, Sl1, K5.
Row 19: With CC, K4, (Sl1, K1) to end.
Row 20: With CC, (K1, Sl1) to last 4 sts, K4.
Row 21: With MC, K5, Sl1, K2, (K3, Sl1, K1, Sl1, K3, Sl1, K2) to last 2 sts, K2.
Row 22: With MC, K2, (K2, Sl1, K3, Sl1, K1, Sl1, K3) to last 8 sts, K2, Sl1, K5.
Row 23: With CC, K4, (Sl1, K1) two times *K8, (Sl1, K1) two times; rep from * to last 2 sts, Sl1, K1.
Row 24: With CC, K1, Sl1, *(K1, Sl1) two times, K8; rep from * to last 8 sts, (K1, Sl1) two times, K4.

Motif Chart (flat over 13 sts)

Row 1 (RS): With CC, K6, Sl1, K1, Sl1, K4.
Row 2 (WS): With CC, K4, Sl1, K1, Sl1, K6.
Row 3: With MC, K7, Sl1, K5.
Row 4: With MC, K5, Sl1, K7.
Row 5: With CC, K4, (Sl1, K1) three times, K3.
Row 6: With CC, K4, (Sl1, K1) three times, K3.
Row 7: With MC, K5, (Sl1, K1) two times, K4.
Row 8: With MC, K5, (Sl1, K1) two times, K4.
Row 9: With CC, Sl1, K9, Sl1, K2.
Row 10: With CC, K2, Sl1, K9, Sl1.
Row 11: With MC, K5, (Sl1, K1) two times, K4.
Row 12: With MC, K5, (Sl1, K1) two times, K4.
Row 13: With CC, K2, Sl1, K9, Sl1.
Row 14: With CC, Sl1, K9, Sl1, K2.
Row 15: With MC, K5, (Sl1, K1) two times, K4.
Row 16: With MC, K5, (Sl1, K1) two times, K4.
Row 17: With CC, K4, (Sl1, K1) three times, K3.
Row 18: With CC, K4, (Sl1, K1) three times, K3.
Row 19: With MC, K5, Sl1, K7.
Row 20: With MC, K7, Sl1, K5.
Row 21: With CC, K4, (Sl1, K1) two times, K5.
Row 22: With CC, K6, (Sl1, K1) two times, K3.

Border Chart

Row 1 (RS): With CC, YO, K2, (K4, Sl1, K1, Sl1, K5) to last 2 sts, K2. 209 sts.
Row 2 (WS): With CC, K2, (K5, Sl1, K1, Sl1, K4) to last 3 sts, K2, K1 TBL.
Row 3: With MC, YO, K7, (K1, Sl1, K10) 13 times, K1, Sl1, K3, Sl1, K1, Sl1, (K5, Sl1, K3, Sl1, K1, Sl1) three times, K2. 210 sts.
Row 4: With MC, K2, (Sl1, K1, Sl1, K3, Sl1, K5) three times, Sl1, K1, Sl1, K3, Sl1, K1, (K10, Sl1, K1) 13 times, K7, K1 TBL.
Row 5: With CC, YO, K6, Sl1, K1, (Sl1, K1, Sl1, K7, Sl1, K1) 13 times, (Sl1, K1) to end. 211 sts.
Row 6: With CC, (K1, Sl1) 23 times, (K1, Sl1, K7, Sl1, K1, Sl1) 13 times, K1, Sl1, K6, K1 TBL.
Row 7: With MC, YO, K8, Sl1, (K1, Sl1, K9, Sl1) 13 times, K1, Sl1, K3, Sl1, K2, (K3, Sl1, K1, Sl1, K3, Sl1, K2) three times, K2. 212 sts.
Row 8: With MC, K2, (K2, Sl1, K3, Sl1, K1, Sl1, K3) three times, K2, Sl1, K3, Sl1, K1, (Sl1, K9, Sl1, K1) 13 times, Sl1, K8, K1 TBL.
Row 9: With CC, YO, K4, Sl1, K1, *K8, (Sl1, K1) two times; rep from * 16 more times, Sl1, K1. 213 sts.

Row 10: With CC, K1, Sl1, *(K1, Sl1) two times, K8; rep from * 16 more times, K1, Sl1, K4, K1 TBL.
Row 11: With MC, YO, K7, (K3, Sl1, K1, Sl1, K6) 17 times, K2. 214 sts.
Row 12: With MC, K2, (K6, Sl1, K1, Sl1, K3) 17 times, K7, K1 TBL.
Row 13: With CC, YO; K4, (Sl1, K1) two times, (Sl1, K9, Sl1, K1) 17 times, Sl1, K1. 215 sts.
Row 14: With CC, K1, Sl1, (K1, Sl1, K9, Sl1) 17 times, (K1, Sl1) two times, K4, K1 TBL.
Row 15: With MC, YO, K8, Sl1, (K3, Sl1, K1, Sl1, K5, Sl1) 17 times, K2. 216 sts.
Row 16: With MC, K2, (Sl1, K5, Sl1, K1, Sl1, K3) 17 times, Sl1, K8, K1 TBL.
Row 17: With CC, YO, K4, (Sl1, K1) to end. 217 sts.
Row 18: With CC, (K1, Sl1) to last 5 sts, K4, K1 TBL.
Row 19: With MC, YO, K8, Sl1, K1, Sl1, (K3, Sl1, K5, Sl1, K1, Sl1) 17 times, K2. 218 sts.
Row 20: With MC, K2, (Sl1, K1, Sl1, K5, Sl1, K3) 17 times, Sl1, K1, Sl1, K8, K1 TBL.
Row 21: With CC, YO, K4, Sl1, K7, (K2, Sl1, K1, Sl1, K7) 17 times, K2. 219 sts.
Row 22: With CC, K2, (K7, Sl1, K1, Sl1, K2) 17 times, K7, Sl1, K4, K1 TBL.
Row 23: With MC, YO, K10, Sl1, K1, Sl1, (K9, Sl1, K1, Sl1) 17 times, K2. 220 sts.
Row 24: With MC, K2, (Sl1, K1, Sl1, K9) 17 times, Sl1, K1, Sl1, K10, K1 TBL.
Row 25: With CC, YO, K4, (Sl1, K1) three times, K4, (K4, Sl1, K1, Sl1, K5) 17 times, K2. 221 sts.
Row 26: With CC, K2, (K5, Sl1, K1, Sl1, K4) 17 times, K5, (Sl1, K1) three times, K3, K1 TBL.
Row 27: With MC, YO, K12, Sl1, K1, Sl1, (K9, Sl1, K1, Sl1) 17 times, K2. 222 sts.
Row 28: With MC, K2, (Sl1, K1, Sl1, K9) 17 times, Sl1, K1, Sl1, K12, K1 TBL.
Row 29: With CC, YO, K4, (Sl1, K1) to end. 223 sts.
Row 30: With CC, (K1, Sl1) to last 5 sts, K4, K1 TBL.
Row 31: With MC, YO, K5, (K9, Sl1, K2) 18 times, K2. 224 sts.
Row 32: With MC, K2, (K2, Sl1, K9) 18 times, K5, K1 TBL.

DIRECTIONS

Setup

With MC, CO 2 sts.
Row 1 (WS): K across.
Join CC.
Row 2 (RS): With CC, KFB, K1. 3 sts.
Row 3: With CC, K across.
Work from Setup Chart or follow written instructions.
Work Rows 1–46. 26 sts.
Rep Rows 23–46 once. 38 sts.
Rep Rows 23–36 once more. 45 sts.

Body

Row 1 (RS): With MC, YO, K7, (K3, Sl1, K1, Sl1, K6) three times, K2. 46 sts.
Row 2 (WS): With MC, K2, (K6, Sl1, K1, Sl1, K3) three times, K7, K1 TBL.

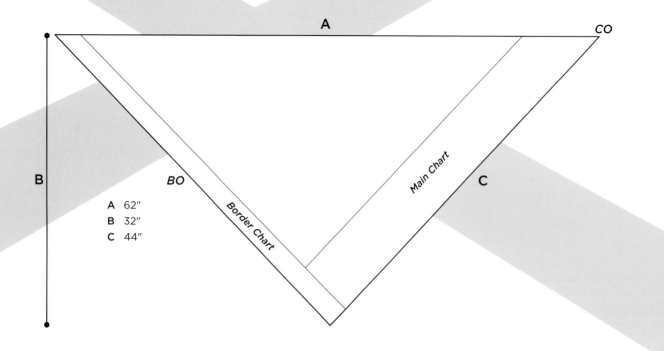

A 62"
B 32"
C 44"

Row 3: With CC, YO, PM, work Row 3 from Main Chart or follow written instructions to end. 47 sts.
Row 4: With CC, work next Row from Main Chart to M, K1 TBL.
Row 5: With MC, YO, K to M, work Main Chart to end. 48 sts.
Row 6: With MC, work Main Chart to M, K to last st, K1 TBL.
Rep Rows 5–6 using CC and MC as needed through Main Chart Row 24. 57 sts.
Rep Main Chart Rows 1–24 two more times. 81 sts.
Rep Main Chart Rows 1–14. 88 sts.

First Motif Insertion
Row 1 (RS): With CC, YO, K12, PM, work from Motif Chart or follow written instructions, PM, K to M, work Row 15 of Main Chart to end. 89 sts.
Row 2 (WS): With CC, work Main Chart to M, K to M, work Motif Chart to M, K to last st, K1 TBL.
Cont as established through Row 22 of Motif Chart. Remove motif markers on last row. 99 sts.
Next Row (RS): With MC, K to M, work subsequent row from Main Chart to end. 1 st inc.
Next Row (WS): Work Main Chart to M, K to last st, K1 TBL.
Rep last two rows twelve more times. 112 sts.

Second Motif Insertion
Rep First Motif Insertion. 136 sts.

Third Motif Insertion
Row 1 (RS): With CC, YO, K12, PM, work from Motif Chart or follow written instructions, PM, K35, PM, work Motif Chart, PM, K to M, work Row 15 from Main Chart to end. 137 sts.
Row 2 (WS): With CC, work Main Chart to M, (K to M, work Motif Chart to M) two times, K to last st, K1 TBL.
Cont as established through Row 22 of Motif Chart. Remove motif markers on last row. 147 sts.

Next Row (RS): With MC, YO, K to M, work subsequent row from Main Chart to end. 1 st inc.
Next Row (WS): Work Main Chart to M, K to last st, K1 TBL.
Rep last two rows twelve more times. 160 sts.

Fourth Motif Insertion
Rep Third Motif Insertion. 184 sts.

Fifth Motif Insertion
Row 1 (RS): With CC, YO, K12, (PM, work from Motif Chart or follow written instructions, PM, K35) two times, PM, work from Motif Chart, PM, K to M, work Row 15 from Main Chart to end. 185 sts.
Row 2 (WS): With CC, work Main Chart to M, (K to M, work Motif Chart to M) three times, K to last st, K1 TBL.
Cont as established through Row 22 of Motif Chart. Remove motif markers on last row. 195 sts.
Next Row (RS): With MC, K to M, work subsequent row from Main Chart to end. 1 st inc.
Next Row (WS): Work Main Chart to M, K to last st, K1 TBL.
Rep last two rows twelve more times. 208 sts.

Border
Work from Border Chart or follow written instructions, through Row 32.
BO as follows: With MC, K1, *bring MC over RH needle from back to front, with CC, K1, pass first and second sts over third st on RH needle, bring CC over RH needle from back to front, with MC, K1, pass first and second sts over third st on RH needle; rep from * to end.
Break yarn and pull through the last st.

Finishing
Weave in ends, wash, and block to diagram.

LEGEND

☐ Main Color

▨ Contrasting Color

◼ **No Stitch**
Placeholder—no stitch made

☐ **K**
RS: Knit stitch
WS: Purl stitch

⦁ **P**
RS: Purl stitch
WS: Knit stitch

Ⅴ **SI**
RS: Slip stitch purl-wise, with yarn in back
WS: Slip stitch purl-wise, with yarn in front

◯ **YO**
Yarn over

Ⓑ **P TBL**
RS: Purl stitch through the back loop
WS: Knit stitch through the back loop

☐ Pattern Repeat

☐ Work 3 Times

☐ Work 13 Times

Setup Chart

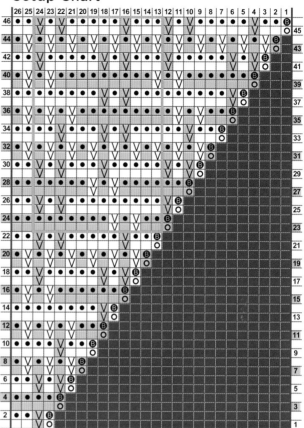

Main Chart

Motif Chart

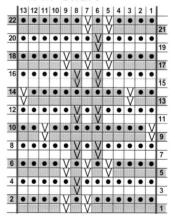

Border Chart

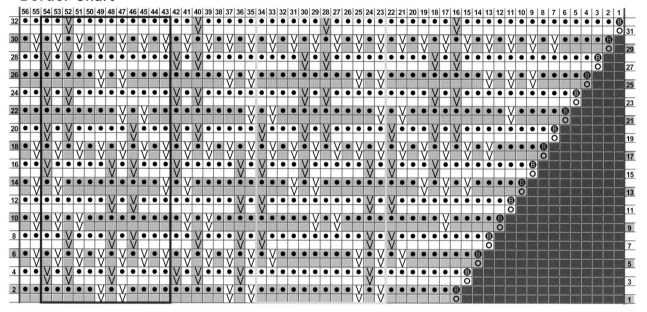

LATERAL SWAY

by Claire Slade

FINISHED MEASUREMENTS
60″ length × 18″ width at widest point

YARN
Chroma™ (fingering weight, 70%
Superwash Wool, 30% Nylon; 396
yards/100g): Pixie 28036, 2 balls

NEEDLES
US 6 (4mm) straight or circular needles
(24–32″), or size to obtain gauge

NOTIONS
Yarn Needle
Blocking Pins and/or Wires

GAUGE
17 sts and 27 rows = 4″ in Sway Pattern,
blocked (gauge is not crucial, but it will
affect finished size and yardage
requirements)

For pattern support, contact verilyknits@gmail.com

Lateral Sway

Notes:

Lateral Sway is Garter Stitch heaven, a deceptively simple-to-knit wrap that has the added bonus of being completely reversible. The rows of offset rings create wonderful swaying edges and an undulating center panel.

This wrap is knit from end to end in one piece. The pattern can be worked from either the charted or written instructions. It is important to ensure that the triple yarn over is always worked *K1, P1, K1* on the wrong side. On completion, the wrap needs to be vigorously blocked to open out the lace pattern.

Sway Pattern is both written and charted. Chart is worked flat; read RS rows (odd numbers) from right to left, and WS rows (even numbers) from left to right.

YO3 (triple yarn over)
Wrap yarn around needle three times.

Sway Pattern (worked flat)
Row 1 (RS): K2, (YO, K3, YO, K2tog, K3, K2tog) two times, YO, K3, YO, K2tog, K6, YO, K2tog, K3, K2tog, YO, K6, (K2tog, YO, K3, YO, K2tog, K3) two times, K2tog, YO, K3, YO, K2. 75 sts.
Row 2 (WS): K across.
Row 3: K2, (YO, K5, YO, K2tog, K1, K2tog) two times, YO, K5, YO, K2tog, K6, YO, K2tog, K1, K2tog, YO, K6, (K2tog, YO, K5, YO, K2tog, K1) two times, K2tog, YO, K5, YO, K2. 77 sts.
Row 4: K across.
Row 5: K2, (YO, K1, K3tog, YO3, K2tog, K1, YO, SK2P) two times, YO, K1, K3tog, YO3, K2tog, K1, YO, K2tog, K6, YO, SK2P, YO, K6, K2tog, (YO, K1, K3tog, YO3, K2tog, K1, YO, SK2P) two times, YO, K1, K3tog, YO3, K2tog, K1, YO, K2. 79 sts.
Row 6: K6, (P1, K9) two times, P1, K25, (P1, K9) two times, P1, K6.

Row 7: K1, K2tog, (YO, K2tog, K3, K2tog, YO, K3) two times, YO, K2tog, K3, K2tog, YO, K6, K2tog, YO, K3, YO, K2tog, K6, (YO, K2tog, K3, K2tog, YO, K3) two times, YO, K2tog, K3, K2tog, YO, K2tog, K1. 77 sts.
Row 8: K across.
Row 9: K1, K2tog, (YO, K2tog, K1, K2tog, YO, K5) two times, YO, K2tog, K1, K2tog, YO, K6, K2tog, YO, K5, YO, K2tog, K6, (YO, K2tog, K1, K2tog, YO, K5) two times, YO, K2tog, K1, K2tog, YO, K2tog, K1. 75 sts.
Row 10: K across.
Row 11: K1, K2tog, (YO, SK2P, YO, K1, K3tog, YO3, K2tog, K1) two times, YO, SK2P, YO, K6, K2tog, YO, K1, K3tog, YO3, K2tog, K1, YO, K2tog, K6, (YO, SK2P, YO, K1, K3tog, YO3, K2tog, K1) two times, YO, SK2P, YO, K2tog, K1. 73 sts.
Row 12: K8, P1, K9, (P1, K17) two times, P1, K9, P1, K8.
Rep Rows 1–12 for pattern.

DIRECTIONS
Loosely CO 73 sts.
Knit two rows.
Work Rows 1–12 of Sway pattern 33 times.
Work Rows 1–10 of Sway pattern once.
Knit two rows.
Loosely BO all sts.

Finishing
Weave in ends, wash, and block to diagram, keeping the CO and BO edges straight and pulling the long sides into gentle waves.

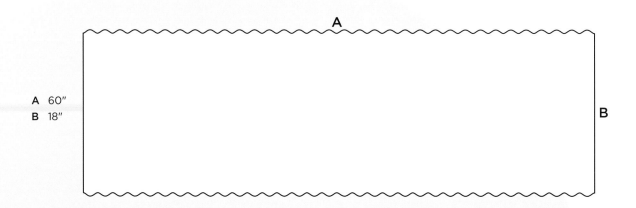

A 60"
B 18"

LEGEND

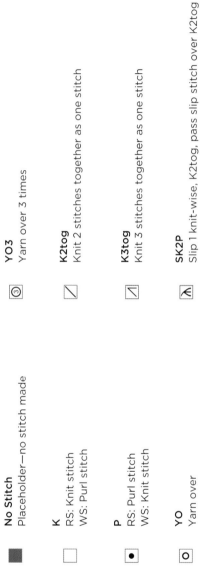

No Stitch
Placeholder—no stitch made

K
RS: Knit stitch
WS: Purl stitch

P
RS: Purl stitch
WS: Knit stitch

YO
Yarn over

YO3
Yarn over 3 times

K2tog
Knit 2 stitches together as one stitch

K3tog
Knit 3 stitches together as one stitch

SK2P
Slip 1 knit-wise, K2tog, pass slip stitch over K2tog

Sway Pattern

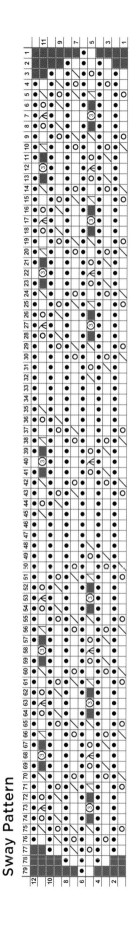

MICHELINA

by Jenny Williams

FINISHED MEASUREMENTS
16.5" depth × 10.25" width at narrowest part, 54" width at widest part

YARN
Stroll™ Tweed (fingering weight, 65% Fine Superwash Merino Wool, 25% Nylon, 10% Donegal; 231 yards/50g): MC Dalmatian 28188, 2 skeins; CC Barley Heather 28194, 1 skein

NEEDLES
US 4 (3.5mm) 32" or longer circular needles, or size to obtain gauge
US 3 (3.25 mm) 32" or longer circular needles, or size to obtain gauge
US 2 (2.75 mm) 32" or longer circular needles, or two sizes smaller than size used to obtain Lace Edging gauge

NOTIONS
Yarn Needle
Locking Stitch Marker
Blocking Pins and Wires
Crochet Hook (for attaching tassels)

GAUGE
25 sts and 18 rows = 4" in Lace Edging with largest needles, lightly blocked
21 sts and 32 rows = 4" in Stockinette Stitch with middle-sized needles, lightly blocked

For pattern support, contact jennyw@tcworks.net

Michelina

Notes:

Michelina is a flirty, crescent-shaped shawl decorated with pops of contrasting color. Surprisingly simple stitches make this an impressive addition to any wardrobe.

The Michelina shawl is worked flat, from the bottom up. A contrasting color cast on (with tassels added at the end) sets the stage. A simple, two-row chevron lace pattern follows, creating a lovely fan. Staccato wrapped stitches are bordered above and below by an eyelet sequence. The remainder of the shawl is worked in Stockinette Stitch short rows, giving it a gentle crescent shape.

Lace Edging (flat over a multiple of 12 sts plus 3)
Row 1 (RS): K2, (YO, K4, SK2P, K4, YO, K1) to last st, K1.
Row 2 (WS): P across.
Rep Rows 1–2 for pattern.

Eyelet Border (flat over a multiple of 2 sts plus 3)
Row 1 (RS): K across.
Row 2 (WS): K across.
Row 3: K1, (K2tog, YO) to last 2 sts, K2.
Row 4: K across.

I-Cord Bind Off
A tutorial for the I-Cord Bind Off can be found at tutorials.knitpicks.com/i-cord-bind-off.

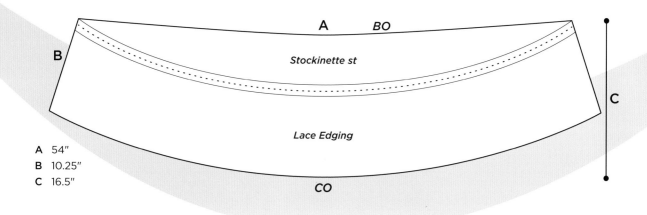

A 54"
B 10.25"
C 16.5"

DIRECTIONS

Lace Edging
With largest needles and CC, CO 363 sts.
Purl one row. Break CC.
Next Row (RS): With MC, work Row 1 of Lace Edging 30 times across row.
Work Row 2 of Lace Edging.
Rep Rows 1–2 of Lace Edging 15 more times.
Change to smallest needles and work Rows 1–2 of Lace Edging once more.

Middle Band
With CC, work Rows 1–4 of Eyelet Border. Break CC.
Next Row (RS): With MC, K1, K2tog, YO, K to last 3 sts, YO, SKP, K1.
Next Row (WS): With MC, P across.
Rep last two rows one more time.

Wrapped Row (RS): With MC, K1, K2tog, YO, K3, *Sl3 to CN, with CC wrap CN sts at the base nine times counter-clockwise, Sl3 from CN to RH needle and carry CC in back, with MC, K3; rep from * to last 6 sts, K3, YO, SKP, K1.
Next Row (WS): With MC, P across.
Next Row (RS): With MC, K1, K2tog, YO, K to last 3 sts, YO, SKP, K1.

Next Row: With MC, P across.
With CC, work Rows 1–4 of Eyelet Border.

Stockinette Body
Dec Row (RS): With middle-sized needles and MC, K1, K2tog, YO, K2, (K2, K2tog) to last 6 sts, K3, YO, SKP, K1. 275 sts.
Purl one row.
Attach locking M to midpoint st—138th st.

Short Rows
Short Row 1 (RS): K1, K2tog, YO, K to 4 sts past M, turn.
Short Row 2 (WS): Sl1 P-wise, P to 4 sts past M, turn.
Short Row 3: Sl1 K-wise, K to 1 st before gap made from turning, SKP, K4, turn. 1 st dec.
Short Row 4: Sl1 P-wise, P to 1 st before gap made from turning, P2tog, P4, turn. 1 st dec.
Rep Short Rows 3–4 25 more times. 223 sts.
Break MC.
Next Short Row (RS): With CC, Sl1 K-wise, K to 1 st before gap made from turning, SKP, YO, SKP, turn.
Next Short Row (WS): Sl1 P-wise, P to 1 st before gap made from turning, P2tog, P2.

I-Cord Bind Off

CO 3 additional sts to LH needle.
Using I-Cord Bind Off, BO all sts.

Finishing

Weave in ends.

Blocking

Even though the gauge swatches were lightly blocked,
the shawl itself should be stretched more because there
will be considerable bounce back on the piece as a whole.
Immerse in cool water for 15 minutes. Gently press out water.

Using blocking pins, pin to diagram measurements. Pull CO
edge to sharp points at SK2Ps. To straighten first Eyelet
Border, pin at the top of each SK2P sequence. Allow to
dry thoroughly.

Tassel Fringe

With CC, cut 10 strands of yarn twice the length desired, plus
1" for knotting. Insert a crochet hook from back to front at
Lace Edging point. Hook folded yarn onto crochet hook, pull
through the knitting and stop. Pull cut ends through folded
loops and pull tight. Rep for each point. Trim ends even.

NEUTRON STAR

by Mary Hull

FINISHED MEASUREMENTS
60.5" width × 25.5" depth; 2.5" center spine width

YARN
Hawthorne™ (fingering weight, 80% Fine Superwash Highland Wool, 20% Polyamide (Nylon); 357 yards/100g): MC Blueberry Speckle 27219, C1 Vancouver Multi 26428, C2 Lovejoy Multi 26865, 1 hank each

NEEDLES
US 5 (3.75mm) 24–32" circular needles, or size to obtain gauge

NOTIONS
Yarn Needle
Two Stitch Markers
Blocking Pins and/or Wires

GAUGE
24 sts and 26 rows = 4" in Garter Stitch, blocked gently

For pattern support, contact kinoknits@gmail.com

Neutron Star

Notes:

It's fun to find new ways to combine colors and tweak traditional shawl shapes. This shawl is structured like a standard symmetrical triangle, but with a wide spine to highlight bubbles of color reminiscent of neutron stars— small, dense celestial bodies—meaning the shawl doesn't come to a sharp point.

Despite the complicated-looking colorwork, only one color is used at a time, so there's no complicated color management. This shawl is so visually striking, it doesn't need a fancy border; you can knit until you run out of yarn, maximizing yardage.

Carrying Yarn

At the start of each RS row, twist working yarn with non-working yarns to catch them and carry them up the edge. This avoids having to break yarn and weave in ends with every stripe.

K4B (knit 4 below)

Insert RH needle into st 4 rows below the next st on LH needle (this will be the last MC st below the next st on LH needle). Carefully drop all 4 sts down to that spot and then knit through the st as you normally would.

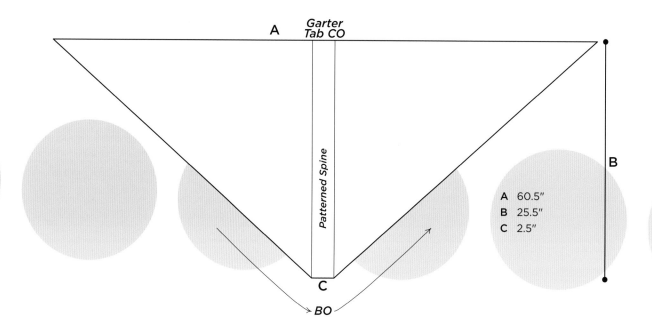

A 60.5"
B 25.5"
C 2.5"

DIRECTIONS

Garter Tab Cast On

With MC, CO 2 sts.
Knit 32 rows. On last row, do not turn work.
Rotate work 90 degrees; PU and K 15 sts, 1 in each Garter ridge. Rotate work 90 degrees; PU and K 2 sts into original cast on sts. 19 sts.

Shawl Body

Setup Row (WS): With MC, K3, PM, P13, PM, K3.
Row 1 (RS): With C1, K2, YO, K to M, YO, SM, K to M, SM, YO, K to last 2 sts, YO, K1, P1. 4 sts inc.
Row 2: With C1, K to M, P to M, K to last st, P1.
Rows 3-4: With C1, rep Rows 1-2. 4 sts inc.
Row 5: With MC, K2, YO, K to M, YO, SM, (K4B, K3) three times, K4B, SM, YO, K to last 2 sts, YO, K1, P1. 4 sts inc.
Row 6: With MC, rep Row 2.
Rows 7-10: With C2, rep Rows 1-4. 8 sts inc.

Row 11: With MC, K2, YO, K to M, YO, SM, K2, (K4B, K3) two times, K4B, K2, SM, YO, K to last 2 sts, YO, K1, P1. 4 sts inc.
Row 12: With MC, rep Row 2.
Rep Rows 1-12 until yarn is almost all used up, or until shawl is desired size, ending with a Row 5 or Row 11. (Sample was made with 16 full reps, then Rows 1-5 worked once more.) Break C1 and C2.

Border

Border Row (WS): With MC, K all sts, removing all markers. With MC, BO all sts.

Finishing

Weave in all ends, wash, and block using blocking wires and pins to shape. Do not stretch the shawl aggressively so that the Garter Stitch remains squishy.

THE OTHER SIDE OF LIFE

by Margaret Mills

FINISHED MEASUREMENTS
8.25" width × 69.5" length, excluding fringe

YARN
Stroll™ (fingering weight, 75% Fine Superwash Merino Wool, 25% Nylon; 231 yards/50g): MC Dove Heather 25023, 3 skeins

and

Stroll™ Tonal Mini Pack (fingering weight, 75% Fine Superwash Merino Wool, 25% Nylon; 462 yards/100g): C1–5 Sunset 44544, 1 pack (C1 Wine Tasting, C2 Heartfelt, C3 Poppy Field, C4 Pansy, C5 Cordial)

NEEDLES
US 4 (3.25mm) 42" or longer circular needles, or size to obtain gauge

NOTIONS
Yarn Needle
13 Stitch Markers
Blocking Pins and/or Wires

GAUGE
24 sts and 48 rows = 4" in Garter Stitch, blocked (note that a larger gauge than this will limit the amount of C1 yarn remaining for tassels)

For pattern support, contact margaretgracemills@gmail.com

The Other Side of Life

Notes:

Explore the other side of a gradient pack with these intriguing stripes! This scarf uses a bit of geometry and a bunch of short rows to take Garter Stitch in a new direction.

The Other Side of Life scarf is knit flat in one piece from one long edge to the other using only one color at a time, with fringe that matches the stripe colors added at the end.

Slip all stitches purl-wise with yarn in front.

BYO (backwards yarn over)

Wrap yarn from back over RH needle to front, then between needles to back. 1 st inc.

Sewn Bind Off

Thread yarn onto a yarn needle. *Insert yarn needle P-wise into first 2 sts on LH needle, pull yarn through but leave sts on LH needle; insert yarn needle K-wise into first st on LH needle, pull yarn through and remove st from LH needle; rep from * until all sts have been removed from LH needle.

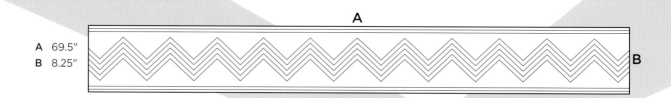

A 69.5"
B 8.25"

DIRECTIONS

Long Edge

With C1 and Long Tail Cast On, CO 417 sts.

Row 1 (WS): Sl1, K to end.

Break C1.

With MC, knit two rows, slipping first st of each row.

With C2, knit four rows, slipping first st of each row.

Break C2.

With MC, knit two rows, slipping first st of each row.

With C3, knit four rows, slipping first st of each row.

Break C3.

Next Row (RS): With MC, Sl1, K to end.

Starting Triangles

Triangles are worked entirely in MC.

Setup Row (WS): Sl1, K10, (PM, K36) eleven times, PM, K10.

First Small Triangle

Short Row 1 (RS): Sl1, K to M, turn.

Short Row 2 and all WS rows: K to end.

Short Row 3: Sl1, K to 1 st before M, turn.

Short Row 5: Sl1, K to 2 sts before M, turn.

Cont as established until only 2 sts are worked on WS row.

Transition Short Row (RS): Sl1, (KFB, K1) four times, K1; SM, do not turn. 4 sts inc.

Full Triangle

Short Row 1 (RS): Sl1, K to M, turn.

Short Row 2 (WS): Sl1, K to 1 st before M, turn.

Short Row 3: Rep Row 2.

Short Row 4: Sl1, K to 2 sts before M, turn.

Short Row 5: Rep Row 4.

Cont as established until only 1 st is worked on WS row.

Transition Short Row (RS): Sl1, KFB, K2, (KFB, K1) five times, K1, KFB, K2; SM, do not turn. 7 sts inc.

Rep Full Triangle ten more times.

Last Small Triangle

Short Row 1 and all RS rows: K to end.

Short Row 2 (WS): Sl1, K to 1 st before M, turn.

Short Row 4: Sl1, K to 2 st before M, turn.

Cont as established until only 2 sts are worked on RS row, ending with a RS row. 498 sts.

Zigzags

Setup Row (WS): Sl1, PM, K1, YO, (KFB, K1) four times, *CDD (removing M), K23, BYO, PM, K1, YO, KFB, K2, (KFB, K1) five times, K1, KFB, K1; rep from * ten more times, CDD (removing M), K to 2 st before end, BYO, PM, K2. 579 sts.

Row 1 (RS): With C4, Sl1, K1, (SM, K1 TFL, K to 2 sts before M, K1 TBL, K1) twelve times, SM, K1.

Row 2 (WS): Sl1, SM, K1, YO, K11, (CDD, K23, BYO, SM, K1, YO, K23) eleven times, CDD, K11, BYO, SM, K2.

Row 3: Rep Row 1.

Row 4: Rep Row 2.

Break C4.

With MC, rep Rows 1–2.
With C5, rep Rows 1–4. Break C5.
With MC, rep Rows 1–2.
With C1, rep Rows 1–4. Break C1.
With MC, rep Rows 1–2.
With C2, rep Rows 1–4. Break C2.
With MC, rep Rows 1–2.
With C3, rep Rows 1–4. Break C3.
With MC, rep Row 1.

Ending Triangles

Triangles are worked entirely in MC.

Setup Row (WS): Sl1, SM, K1, YO, (K2tog, K1) three times, K2tog, *CDD, K to M, BYO, SM, K1, YO, (K1, K2tog) six times, K2, K2tog, K1; rep from * ten more times, CDD, K to M, BYO, SM, K2. 498 sts.

First Partial Triangle

Transition Short Row (RS): Sl1, K1, SM, (K2tog, K1) four times, turn. 4 sts dec.

Short Row 1 (WS): K1, turn.

Short Row 2 (RS): K2, turn.

Cont to work 1 st more each short row until WS row reaches M, remove M, turn.

Short Row 18 (RS): K18, turn.

Short Row 19 and all remaining WS rows: K to end.

Short Row 20: Sl1, K20.

Short Row 22: Sl1, K21.

Cont to work 1 st more each RS short row until RS row ends 2 sts from M.

Next RS Short Row: Sl1, K26, K1 TBL, turn.

Next RS Short Row: Sl1, K to M; SM, do not turn.

Full Triangle

Transition Short Row (RS): K1 TFL, K1, K2tog, K2, (K2tog, K1) six times, K1, turn. 7 sts dec.

Short Row 1 (WS): K1, turn.

Short Row 2 (RS): K2, turn.

Cont to work 1 st more each short row until WS ends 1 st from M, turn.

Next Short Row (RS): K33, K1 TBL, turn.

Next Short Row (WS): K to M, remove M, turn.

Next Short Row: K to M; SM, do not turn.

Rep Full Triangle nine more times.

Last Partial Triangle

Transition Short Row (RS): K1 TFL, K1, K2tog, K2, (K2tog, K1) six times, K1, turn. 7 sts dec.

Short Row 1 (WS): K1, turn.

Short Row 2 (RS): K2, turn.

Cont to work 1 st more each short row until RS row ends 2 sts from M, turn.

Short Row 15 (WS): K15, turn.

Short Row 16 (RS): K15, K1 TBL, turn.

Short Row 17: K17, turn.

Short Row 18: K to M, remove M, K1.

Short Row 19: Sl1, K19, turn.

Short Row 20 and all remaining RS rows: K to end.

Short Row 21: Sl1, K20, turn.

Short Row 23: Sl1, K21, turn.

Cont to work 1 st more each WS short row until WS row ends at M, remove M, turn.

Next Short Row: K to end. 417 sts.

Long Edge

Setup Row (WS): With MC, Sl1, K to end.
With C4, knit four rows, slipping first st of each row.
Break C4.
With MC, knit two rows, slipping first st of each row.
With C5, knit four rows, slipping first st of each row.
Break C5.
With MC, knit two rows, slipping first st of each row.
Break MC.
With C1, knit two rows, slipping first st of each row.
Break C1, leaving a tail approx 4 feet long (or length you can work with comfortably).

With RS facing, BO all sts using Sewn Bind Off. Work until yarn tail is 3–4″ long. Cut another piece of yarn and cont working BO until all sts have been bound off.

Finishing

Weave in ends, wash, and block to diagram.

Tassels

Cut three pieces of C1 yarn each 10″ long. Using a yarn needle or crochet hook, insert them in one bundle along short edge of scarf, 2 sts from edge at one end of C1 garter ridge. Gather all yarn ends tog and tie in a neat overhand knot. Make a matching tassel at end of C1 garter ridge on other short edge.

Make a tassel at end of all other contrast color stripes, using six strands of matching contrast color. Using a yarn needle or hook, insert them at end of each stripe. Gather all yarn ends tog and tie each in a neat overhand knot.

Make four MC tassels on either side of CC zigzags, evenly spaced between zigzags and long-edge stripes, using five strands of MC in each tassel.

Rep all tassels along other short edge of scarf.
Trim all tassels to even ends.

PLAYFULLY

by Mone Dräger

FINISHED MEASUREMENTS
48" along top edge, 83.5" along bottom edge × 10" depth (without tassels)

YARN
Stroll™ (fingering weight; 75% Fine Superwash Merino Wool, 25% Nylon; 231 yards/50g): MC Frost 28183, 2 skeins
and
Stroll™ Tonal Mini Pack (fingering weight; 75% Fine Superwash Merino Wool, 25% Nylon; 462 yards/100g): C1–5 Moody Blues 44539, 1 pack (C1 Blue Violet, C2 Orbit, C3 Pansy, C4 Deep Waters, C5 Raven)

NEEDLES
US 2 (3mm) straight or circular needles (24–32"), or size to obtain gauge

NOTIONS
Yarn Needle
Blocking Pins and/or Wires
Small Crochet Hook (to attach tassels)

GAUGE
26 sts and 34 rows = 4" in Garter Stitch, blocked (gauge is not crucial, but it will affect finished size and yardage requirements)

For pattern support, contact mone.draeger@web.de

Playfully

Notes:

Playfully is a versatile accessory, which can be worked with as many colors as desired depending on personal preferences. Use multiple bright colors for a more playful look or work the shawlette with neutrals for a more subdued, elegant look.

The shawlette is knit sideways completely in Garter Stitch. At given intervals, triangle shaped insertions are worked from the bottom edge, creating the crescent shape, using German Short Rows. As the eye-catching finishing touch, tassels are added to all triangles in contrast colors.

To avoid having to sew in multiple yarn ends, the MC can be carried along when working the CC triangles. Twist the MC around the CC yarn at the beginning of every RS row. Make sure to leave MC loose when picking it up again to avoid having the triangles pull together when blocking. If preferred, break MC at each triangle insertion and join again when needed.

DS (double stitch)
Please refer to German Short Rows in Glossary.

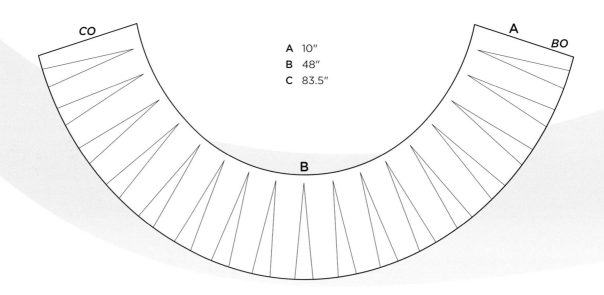

A 10"
B 48"
C 83.5"

DIRECTIONS

With MC, loosely CO 65 sts.
Knit 26 rows.

*Join C1, leaving a tail of approx 6".
Short Row 1 (RS): K54, turn.
Short Row 2 and all WS rows: DS, K to end.
Short Row 3: K43, turn.
Short Row 5: K32, turn.
Short Row 7: K21, turn.
Short Row 9: K10, turn.
Short Row 11: K22, turn.
Short Row 13: K33, turn.
Short Row 15: K44, turn.
Short Row 17: K55, turn.
Short Row 18 (WS): DS, K to end. Break C1, leaving a tail of approx 6".
Pick up (or join) MC and knit 22 rows.

Rep from * 16 more times, using C2, C3, C4, C5, then starting with C1 again and continuing in established color scheme.
Knit four more rows in MC.
BO loosely.

Finishing
Weave in MC ends, wash, and block to diagram.

Tassels
For each triangle, cut 8 strands of yarn of approx 12" in the appropriate color. Use a crochet hook to pull one thread through each of the 7 middle purl bumps of the triangle. Pull thread completely through, so that half of thread is on each side. Gather all threads, including ends from knitting, approx 1" from fabric. Form a loop at one end of remaining thread, wrap loose end around gathered threads and through loop and pull tight, forming a knot. Cont to hold looped end and wrap loose end around tassel six times. Tie the two ends in a knot to secure. Cut all threads to same length of approx 4" total, measured from fabric.

PRISM

by Violet LeBeaux

FINISHED MEASUREMENTS

56 (80)″ width × 14 (18)″ depth from
center to edge of curve (as the shawl
is a combination of Garter Stitch and
ribbing, it is very stretchy until I-Cord
is added to stabilize edge)
Sample is 80×18″ size

YARN

Chroma™ (fingering weight, 70%
Superwash Wool, 30% Nylon; 396
yards/100g): MC Bare 25248, 1 (2)
balls; CC Tiki 28041, 1 ball

NEEDLES

US 6 (4mm) straight or circular needles,
or size to obtain gauge

US 7 (4.5mm) straight or circular
needles, or size to obtain gauge
US 7 (4.5mm) DPNs or circular needles,
or size needed for applied I-Cord edging

NOTIONS

Yarn Needle
Blocking Pins and/or Wires

GAUGE

20 sts and 48 rows = 4″ in Garter Stitch
on smaller needles, blocked
20 sts and 32 rows = 4″ in Corrugated
Ribbing on larger needles, blocked

For pattern support, contact violetlebeaux@gmail.com

Prism

Notes:

Prism is a light and bright crescent shawl. It's a perfect project to compliment rainbow-colored yarns as the neutral main color offsets tonal changes. The result is a wearable way to add a pop of color to any outfit.

The shawl features Garter Stitch, two-tone Rib, applied I-Cord edging, and tassels. Construction is center out with the I-Cord edging and tassels added afterwards. This project is a fun way for beginners to try out stranded ribbing.

Applied I-Cord Edging

I-Cord is a thin tube of knitting that is only a few stitches wide. Applied I-Cord edging uses the same principle with an additional stitch picked up from the edge of your main work every row to secure it.

There are some great tips in this article including working it as a bind off: tutorials.knitpicks.com/i-cord-bind-off.

Corrugated Ribbing

Two-color ribbing involves working knit sts with one color and purl sts with another. The non-working yarn is always carried along the WS of the work. There are great instructions and photos in this tutorial: tutorials.knitpicks.com/ribbing.

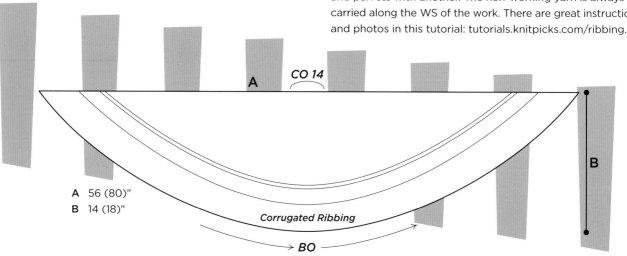

A 56 (80)"
B 14 (18)"

Corrugated Ribbing

→ *BO* →

DIRECTIONS

Body

With MC and smaller needles, loosely CO 14 sts.
Row 1 (RS): K2, M1, K to last 2 sts, M1, K2. 2 sts inc.
With MC, rep Row 1 until there are 66 (126) sts, ending with a WS row. Piece measures approx 5.5 (10.5)" from CO edge at deepest point.
With CC, rep Row 1 two times. 68 (128) sts.
With MC, rep Row 1 six times. 80 (140) sts.
With CC, rep Row 1 two times. 82 (142) sts.
With MC, rep Row 1 until there are 206 (326) sts, ending with a WS row. Piece measures approx 8 (13)" from CO edge at deepest point.

Corrugated Ribbing

Switch to larger needles. Be sure to carry the non-working yarn across the WS.
Row 1 (RS): With MC, K2, M1P; (with CC, K2; with MC, P2) to last 4 sts; with CC, K2; with MC, M1P, K2. 2 sts inc.
Row 2 (WS): With MC, P2, M1, work Rib as established to last 2 sts; with MC, M1, P2. 2 sts inc.
Row 3: With MC, K2; with CC, M1, work as established to last 2 sts; with CC, M1; with MC, K2. 2 sts inc.
Row 4: With MC, P2; with CC, M1P, work as established to last 2 sts; with CC, M1P; with MC, P2. 2 sts inc.
Rep Rows 1–4 seven more times. 270 (390) sts.

Corrugated Ribbing section measures approx 4".
Break CC.
With MC, BO all sts.
Wash and block to shape before moving on to the Applied I-Cord Edging.

Applied I-Cord Edging

An I-Cord edge is worked using MC around the entire shawl. With RS facing, start from a corner and work down straight edge as follows.
With MC, PU and K 1 st from edge of work onto LH needle, CO 3 sts to LH needle.
Rnd 1: K2, Sl1, K1, PSSO, PU and K 1 st from edge of work, Sl all sts from RH needle back to LH needle.
Rep Rnd 1 until entire edge of shawl has been worked.
Work Rnd 1 twice at each corner st to create a crisp point.
Make sure to watch tension when working on curved edge: if I-Cord is too tight it will affect final shape. If this happens, use a larger size needle.
BO all sts and graft or seam CO and BO ends tog.

Finishing

Make two 3" tassels with CC and attach to each shawl point. Weave in ends, wash, and block to diagram.

RECOMBINANT

by M K Nance

FINISHED MEASUREMENTS
70″ circumference × 6″ height

YARN
Stroll™ (fingering weight, 75% Fine Superwash Merino Wool, 25% Nylon; 231 yards/50g): MC Frost 28183, 2 skeins *and*
Stroll™ Gradient (fingering weight, 75% Fine Superwash Merino Wool, 25% Nylon; 458 yards/100g): CC Dragon Breath 28257, 1 cake

NEEDLES
US 3 (3.25mm) 24–32″ circular needles, or size to obtain gauge

NOTIONS
Yarn Needle
Stitch Markers
Cable Needle

GAUGE
19 sts and 60 rnds = 4″ in Two Color Garter Stitch in the round, blocked

For pattern support, contact mknanceknit@gmail.com

Recombinant

Notes:

This is a bold explosion and recombination of traditional argyle motifs. The main panel is offset by Garter Stitch in alternating colors that read from afar as marled. It can be worn as a double or single loop.

The Recombinant cowl features mosaic cables floating over Garter Stitch. The sample was made with a solid MC and the gradient yarn as the CC, but different kinds of color options can also work very well with the pattern.

Cable pattern is both written and charted. Only one yarn color is used for each round—on chart, the color of the round number is the color used on that round. Chart is worked in the round; read each chart row from right to left as a RS row.

LT (left twist)
Sl1 to CN, hold in front; K1, K1 from CN.

RT (right twist)
Sl1 to CN, hold in back; K1, K1 from CN.

1/2 LC (cable 1 over 2 left)
Sl1 to CN, hold in front; K2, K1 from CN.

1/2 RC (cable 1 over 2 right)
Sl2 to CN, hold in back; K1, K2 from CN.

1/1/1 LC (cable 1 over 1 left, with center stitch)
Sl2 to CN, hold in front; K1, Sl center st from CN back to LH needle and knit it; K1 from CN.

1/1/1 RC (cable 1 over 1 right, with center stitch)
Sl2 to CN, hold in back; K1, Sl center st from CN back to LH needle and knit it; K1 from CN.

Two-Color Garter Pattern (worked flat)
Rnd 1: With CC, K all.
Rnd 2: With MC, P all.

Cable Pattern (in the round over 94 sts)
Rnd 1: With CC, K1 TBL, P3, Sl1, P6, Sl1, P4, Sl1, P6, Sl1, P3, Sl1, K37, Sl1, P3, Sl1, P6, Sl1, P4, Sl1, P6, Sl1, P3, K1 TBL, K1.
Rnd 2: In MC, Sl1, K3, LT, K4, RT, K4, LT, K4, RT, K3, K1 TBL, P5, (Sl1, P1, Sl1, P9) two times, Sl1, P1, Sl1, P5, K1 TBL, K3, LT, K4, RT, K4, LT, K4, RT, K3, Sl1, P1.
Rnd 3: With CC, K1 TBL, (P4, Sl1) two times, P6, (Sl1, P4) two times, Sl1, K5, 1/2 LC, K9, 1/1/1 RC, K9, 1/2 RC, K5, Sl1, (P4, Sl1) two times, P6, (Sl1, P4) two times, K1 TBL, K1.
Rnd 4: With MC, Sl1, K4, LT, K2, RT, K6, LT, K2, RT, K4, K1 TBL, P7, Sl1, P9, Sl1, P1, Sl1, P9, Sl1, P7, K1 TBL, K4, LT, K2, RT, K6, LT, K2, RT, K4, Sl1, P1.
Rnd 5: With CC, K1 TBL, P5, Sl1, P2, Sl1, P8, Sl1, P2, Sl1, P5, Sl1, K7, 1/2 LC, K5, 1/2 RC, K1, 1/2 LC, K5, 1/2 RC, K7, Sl1, P5, Sl1, P2, Sl1, P8, Sl1, P2, Sl1, P5, K1 TBL, K1.
Rnd 6: With MC, Sl1, K5, LT, RT, K8, LT, RT, K5, K1 TBL, P9, (Sl1, P5) three times, Sl1, P9, K1 TBL, K5, LT, RT, K8, LT, RT, K5, Sl1, P1.
Rnd 7: With CC, K1 TBL, P6, Sl2, P10, Sl2, P6, Sl1, K9, 1/2 LC, K1, 1/2 RC, K5, 1/2 LC, K1, 1/2 RC, K9, Sl1, P6, Sl2, P10, Sl2, P6, K1 TBL, K1.

Rnd 8: With MC, Sl1, K6, LT, K10, LT, K6, K1 TBL, P11, Sl1, P1, Sl1, P9, Sl1, P1, Sl1, P11, K1 TBL, K6, LT, K10, LT, K6, Sl1, P1.
Rnd 9: With CC, K1 TBL, P6, Sl2, P10, Sl2, P6, Sl1, K11, 1/1/1 LC, K9, 1/1/1 LC, K11, Sl1, P6, Sl2, P10, Sl2, P6, K1 TBL, K1.
Rnd 10: With MC, Sl1, K5, RT, LT, K8, RT, LT, K5, K1 TBL, P11, Sl1, P1, Sl1, P9, Sl1, P1, Sl1, P11, K1 TBL, K5, RT, LT, K8, RT, LT, K5, Sl1, P1.
Rnd 11: With CC, K1 TBL, P5, Sl1, P2, Sl1, P8, Sl1, P2, Sl1, P5, Sl1, K9, 1/2 RC, K1, 1/2 LC, K5, 1/2 RC, K1, 1/2 LC, K9, Sl1, P5, Sl1, P2, Sl1, P8, Sl1, P2, Sl1, P5, K1 TBL, K1.
Rnd 12: With MC, Sl1, K4, RT, K2, LT, K6, RT, K2, LT, K4, K1 TBL, P9, (Sl1, P5) three times, Sl1, P9, K1 TBL, K4, RT, K2, LT, K6, RT, K2, LT, K4, Sl1, P1.
Rnd 13: With CC, K1 TBL, (P4, Sl1) two times, P6, (Sl1, P4) two times, Sl1, K7, 1/2 RC, K5, 1/2 LC, K1, 1/2 RC, K5, 1/2 LC, K7, (Sl1, P4) two times, Sl1, P6, (Sl1, P4) two times, K1 TBL, K1.
Rnd 14: With MC, Sl1, K3, RT, K4, LT, K4, RT, K4, LT, K3, K1 TBL, P7, Sl1, P9, Sl1, P1, Sl1, P9, Sl1, P7, K1 TBL, K3, RT, K4, LT, K4, RT, K4, LT, K3, Sl1, P1.
Rnd 15: With CC, K1 TBL, P3, Sl1, P6, Sl1, P4, Sl1, P6, Sl1, P3, Sl1, K5, 1/2 RC, K9, 1/1/1 RC, K9, 1/2 LC, K5, Sl1, P3, Sl1, P6, Sl1, P4, Sl1, P6, Sl1, P3, K1 TBL, K1.
Rnd 16: With MC, Sl1, (K2, RT, K6, LT) two times, K2, K1 TBL, P5, Sl1, P11, Sl1, P1, Sl1, P11, Sl1, P5, K1 TBL, (K2, RT, K6, LT) two times, K2, Sl1, P1.
Rnd 17: With CC, K1 TBL, (P2, Sl1, P8, Sl1) two times, P2, Sl1, K3, 1/2 RC, K9, 1/2 RC, K1, 1/2 LC, K9, 1/2 LC, K3, (Sl1, P2, Sl1, P8) two times, Sl1, P2, K1 TBL, K1.
Rnd 18: With MC, Sl1, K1, (RT, K8, LT) two times, K1, K1 TBL, P3, Sl1, P11, Sl1, P5, Sl1, P11, Sl1, P3, K1 TBL, K1, (RT, K8, LT) two times, K1, Sl1, P1.
Rnd 19: With CC, K1 TBL, P1, Sl1, P10, Sl2, P10, Sl1, P1, Sl1, K1, 1/2 RC, K9, 1/2 RC, K5, 1/2 LC, K9, 1/2 LC, K1, Sl1, P1, Sl1, P10, Sl2, P10, Sl1, P1, K1 TBL, K1.
Rnd 20: With MC, Sl1, K12, RT, K12, K1 TBL, P1, Sl1, P11, Sl1, P9, Sl1, P11, Sl1, P1, K1 TBL, K12, RT, K12, Sl1, P1.
Rnd 21: With CC, K1 TBL, P1, Sl1, P10, Sl2, P10, Sl1, P1, Sl1, K11, 1/2 RC, K9, 1/2 LC, K11, Sl1, P1, Sl1, P10, Sl2, P10, Sl1, P1, K1 TBL, K1.
Rnd 22: With MC, Sl1, K1, (LT, K8, RT) two times, K1, K1 TBL, P1, Sl1, P9, Sl1, P13, Sl1, P9, Sl1, P1, K1 TBL, K1, (LT, K8, RT) two times, K1, Sl1, P1.
Rnd 23: With CC, K1 TBL, (P2, Sl1, P8, Sl1) two times, P2, Sl1, K9, 1/2 RC, K13, 1/2 LC, K9, Sl1, (P2, Sl1, P8, Sl1) two times, P2, K1 TBL, K1.
Rnd 24: With MC, Sl1, (K2, LT, K6, RT) two times, K2, K1 TBL, P1, Sl1, P7, Sl1, P17, Sl1, P7, Sl1, P1, K1 TBL, (K2, LT, K6, RT) two times, K2, Sl1, P1.
Rnd 25: With CC, K1 TBL, P3, Sl1, P6, Sl1, P4, Sl1, P6, Sl1, P3, Sl1, K7, 1/2 RC, K17, 1/2 LC, K7, Sl1, P3, Sl1, P6, Sl1, P4, Sl1, P6, Sl1, P3, K1 TBL, K1.
Rnd 26: With MC, Sl1, K3, LT, K4, RT, K4, LT, K4, RT, K3, K1 TBL, P1, Sl1, P5, Sl1, P21, Sl1, P5, Sl1, P1, K1 TBL, K3, LT, K4, RT, K4, LT, K4, RT, K3, Sl1, P1.

Rnd 27: With CC, K1 TBL, (P4, Sl1) two times, P6, (Sl1, P4) two times, Sl1, K5, 1/2 RC, K21, 1/2 LC, K5, Sl1, (P4, Sl1) two times, P6, (Sl1, P4) two times, K1 TBL, K1.

Rnd 28: With MC, Sl1, K4, LT, K2, RT, K6, LT, K2, RT, K4, K1 TBL, P1, Sl1, P3, Sl1, P25, Sl1, P3, Sl1, P1, K1 TBL, K4, LT, K2, RT, K6, LT, K2, RT, K4, Sl1, P1.

Rnd 29: With CC, K1 TBL, P5, Sl1, P2, Sl1, P8, Sl1, P2, Sl1, P5, Sl3, 1/2 RC, K25, 1/2 LC, K3, Sl1, P5, Sl1, P2, Sl1, P8, Sl1, P2, Sl1, P5, K1 TBL, K1.

Rnd 30: With MC, Sl1, K5, LT, RT, K8, LT, RT, K5, K1 TBL, (P1, Sl1) two times, P29, (Sl1, P1) two times, K1 TBL, K5, LT, RT, K8, LT, RT, K5, Sl1, P1.

Rnd 31: With CC, K1 TBL, P6, Sl2, P10, Sl2, P6, Sl1, K1, 1/1/1 LC, K29, 1/1/1 RC, K1, Sl1, P6, Sl2, P10, Sl2, P6, K1 TBL, K1.

Rnd 32: With MC, Sl1, K6, RT, K10, LT, K6, K1 TBL, (P1, Sl1) two times, P29, (Sl1, P1) two times, K1 TBL, K6, RT, K10, LT, K6, Sl1, P1.

Rnd 33: With CC, K1 TBL, P6, Sl1, P12, Sl1, P6, Sl1, K3, 1/2 LC, K25, 1/2 RC, K3, Sl1, P6, Sl1, P12, Sl1, P6, K1 TBL, K1.

Rnd 34: With MC, Sl1, K5, RT, K12, LT, K5, K1 TBL, P1, Sl1, P3, Sl1, P25, Sl1, P3, Sl1, P1, K1 TBL, K5, RT, K12, LT, K5, Sl1, P1.

Rnd 35: With CC, K1 TBL, P5, Sl1, P14, Sl1, P5, Sl1, K5, 1/2 LC, K21, 1/2 RC, K5, Sl1, P5, Sl1, P14, Sl1, P5, K1 TBL, K1.

Rnd 36: With MC, Sl1, K4, RT, K14, LT, K4, K1 TBL, P1, Sl1, P5, Sl1, P21, Sl1, P5, Sl1, P1, K1 TBL, K4, RT, K14, LT, K4, Sl1, P1.

Rnd 37: With CC, K1 TBL, P4, Sl1, P16, Sl1, P4, Sl1, K7, 1/2 LC, K17, 1/2 RC, K7, Sl1, P4, Sl1, P16, Sl1, P4, K1 TBL, K1.

Rnd 38: With MC, Sl1, K3, RT, K16, LT, K3, K1 TBL, P1, Sl1, P7, Sl1, P17, Sl1, P7, Sl1, P1, K1 TBL, K3, RT, K16, LT, K3, Sl1, P1.

Rnd 39: With CC, K1 TBL, P3, Sl1, P18, Sl1, P3, Sl1, K9, 1/2 LC, K13, 1/2 RC, K9, Sl1, P3, Sl1, P18, Sl1, P3, K1 TBL, K1.

Rnd 40: With MC, Sl1, K2, RT, K18, LT, K2, K1 TBL, P1, Sl1, P9, Sl1, P13, Sl1, P9, Sl1, P1, K1 TBL, K2, RT, K18, LT, K2, Sl1, P1.

Rnd 41: With CC, K1 TBL, P2, Sl1, P20, Sl1, P2, Sl1, K11, 1/2 LC, K9, 1/2 RC, K11, Sl1, P2, Sl1, P20, Sl1, P2, K1 TBL, K1.

Rnd 42: With MC, Sl1, K1, RT, K20, LT, K1, K1 TBL, P1, Sl1, P11, Sl1, P9, Sl1, P11, Sl1, P1, K1 TBL, K1, RT, K20, LT, K1, Sl1, P1.

Rnd 43: With CC, K1 TBL, P1, Sl1, P22, Sl1, P1, Sl1, K13, 1/2 LC, K5, 1/2 RC, K13, Sl1, P1, Sl1, P22, Sl1, P1, K1 TBL, K1.

Rnd 44: With MC, Sl1, K26, K1 TBL, P1, Sl1, P13, Sl1, P5, Sl1, P13, Sl1, P1, K1 TBL, K26, Sl1, P1.

Rnd 45: With CC, K1 TBL, P1, Sl1, P22, Sl1, P1, Sl1, K37, Sl1, P1, Sl1, P22, Sl1, P1, K1 TBL, K1.

Rnd 46: With MC, Sl1, K1, LT, K20, RT, K1, K1 TBL, P1, Sl1, P13, Sl1, P5, Sl1, P13, Sl1, P1, K1 TBL, K1, LT, K20, RT, K1, Sl1, P1.

Rnd 47: With CC, K1 TBL, P2, Sl1, P20, Sl1, P2, Sl1, K13, 1/2 RC, K5, 1/2 LC, K13, Sl1, P2, Sl1, P20, Sl1, P2, K1 TBL, K1.

Rnd 48: With MC, Sl1, K2, LT, K18, RT, K2, K1 TBL, P1, Sl1, P11, Sl1, P9, Sl1, P11, Sl1, P1, K1 TBL, K2, LT, K18, RT, K2, Sl1, P1.

Rnd 49: With CC, K1 TBL, P3, Sl1, P18, Sl1, P3, Sl1, K11, 1/2 RC, K9, 1/2 LC, K11, Sl1, P3, Sl1, P18, Sl1, P3, K1 TBL, K1.

Rnd 50: With MC, Sl1, K3, LT, K16, RT, K3, K1 TBL, P1, Sl1, P9, Sl1, P13, Sl1, P9, Sl1, P1, K1 TBL, K3, LT, K16, RT, K3, Sl1, P1.

Rnd 51: With CC, K1 TBL, P4, Sl1, P16, Sl1, P4, Sl1, K9, 1/2 RC, K13, 1/2 LC, K9, Sl1, P4, Sl1, P16, Sl1, P4, K1 TBL, K1.

Rnd 52: With MC, Sl1, K4, LT, K14, RT, K4, K1 TBL, P1, Sl1, P7, Sl1, P17, Sl1, P7, Sl1, P1, K1 TBL, K4, LT, K14, RT, K4, Sl1, P1.

Rnd 53: With CC, K1 TBL, P5, Sl1, P14, Sl1, P5, Sl1, K7, 1/2 RC, K17, 1/2 LC, K7, Sl1, P5, Sl1, P14, Sl1, P5, K1 TBL, K1.

Rnd 54: With MC, Sl1, K5, LT, K12, RT, K5, K1 TBL, P1, Sl1, P5, Sl1, P21, Sl1, P5, Sl1, P1, K1 TBL, K5, LT, K12, RT, K5, Sl1, P1.

Rnd 55: With CC, K1 TBL, P6, Sl1, P12, Sl1, P6, Sl1, K5, 1/2 RC, K21, 1/2 LC, K5, Sl1, P6, Sl1, P12, Sl1, P6, K1 TBL, K1.

Rnd 56: With MC, Sl1, K6, LT, K10, RT, K6, K1 TBL, P1, Sl1, P3, Sl1, P25, Sl1, P3, Sl1, P1, K1 TBL, K6, LT, K10, RT, K6, Sl1, P1.

Rnd 57: With CC, K1 TBL, P6, Sl2, P10, Sl2, P6, Sl1, K3, 1/2 RC, K25, 1/2 LC, K3, Sl1, P6, Sl2, P10, Sl2, P6, K1 TBL, K1.

Rnd 58: With MC, Sl1, K5, RT, LT, K8, RT, LT, K5, K1 TBL, (P1, Sl1) two times, P29, (Sl1, P1) two times, K1 TBL, K5, RT, LT, K8, RT, LT, K5, Sl1, P1.

Rnd 59: With CC, K1 TBL, P5, Sl1, P2, Sl1, P8, Sl1, P2, Sl1, P5, Sl1, K1, 1/1/1 RC, K29, 1/1/1 LC, K1, Sl1, P5, Sl1, P2, Sl1, P8, Sl1, P2, Sl1, P5, K1 TBL, K1.

Rnd 60: With MC, Sl1, K4, RT, K2, LT, K6, RT, K2, LT, K4, K1 TBL, (P1, Sl1) two times, P29, (Sl1, P1) two times, K1 TBL, K4, RT, K2, LT, K6, RT, K2, LT, K4, Sl1, P1.

Rnd 61: With CC, K1 TBL, (P4, Sl1) two times, P6, (Sl1, P4) two times, Sl1, K3, 1/2 LC, K25, 1/2 RC, K3, Sl1, (P4, Sl1) two times, P6, (Sl1, P4) two times, K1 TBL, K1.

Rnd 62: With MC, Sl1, K3, RT, K4, LT, K4, RT, K4, LT, K3, K1 TBL, P1, Sl1, P3, Sl1, P25, Sl1, P3, Sl1, P1, K1 TBL, K3, RT, K4, LT, K4, RT, K4, LT, K3, Sl1, P1.

Rnd 63: With CC, K1 TBL, P3, Sl1, P6, Sl1, P4, Sl1, P6, Sl1, P3, Sl1, K5, 1/2 LC, K21, 1/2 RC, K5, Sl1, P3, Sl1, P6, Sl1, P4, Sl1, P6, Sl1, P3, K1 TBL, K1.

Rnd 64: With MC, Sl1, (K2, RT, K6, LT) two times, K2, K1 TBL, P1, Sl1, P5, Sl1, P21, Sl1, P5, Sl1, P1, K1 TBL, (K2, RT, K6, LT) two times, K2, Sl1, P1.

Rnd 65: With CC, K1 TBL, (P2, Sl1, P8, Sl1) two times, P2, Sl1, K7, 1/2 LC, K17, 1/2 RC, K7, (Sl1, P2, Sl1, P8) two times, Sl1, P2, K1 TBL, K1.

Rnd 66: With MC, Sl1, K1, (RT, K8, LT) two times, K1, K1 TBL, P1, Sl1, P7, Sl1, P17, Sl1, P7, Sl1, P1, K1 TBL, K1, (RT, K8, LT) two times, K1, Sl1, P1.

Rnd 67: With CC, K1 TBL, P1, Sl1, P10, Sl2, P10, Sl1, P1, Sl1, K9, 1/2 LC, K13, 1/2 RC, K9, Sl1, P1, Sl1, P10, Sl2, P10, Sl1, P1, K1 TBL, K1.

Rnd 68: With MC, Sl1, K12, RT, K12, K1 TBL, P1, Sl1, P9, Sl1, P13, Sl1, P9, Sl1, P1, K1 TBL, K12, RT, K12, Sl1, P1.

Rnd 69: With CC, K1 TBL, P1, Sl1, P10, Sl2, P10, Sl1, P1, Sl1, K11, 1/2 LC, K9, 1/2 RC, K11, Sl1, P1, Sl1, P10, Sl2, P10, Sl1, P1, K1 TBL, K1.

Rnd 70: With MC, Sl1, K1, (LT, K8, RT) two times, K1, K1 TBL, P1, Sl1, P11, Sl1, P9, Sl1, P11, Sl1, P1, K1 TBL, K1, (LT, K8, RT) two times, K1, Sl1, P1.

Rnd 71: With CC, K1 TBL, (P2, Sl1, P8, Sl1) two times, P2, Sl1, K1, 1/2 LC, K9, 1/2 LC, K5, 1/2 RC, K9, 1/2 RC, K1, Sl1, (P2, Sl1, P8, Sl1) two times, P2, K1 TBL, K1.

Rnd 72: With MC, Sl1, (K2, LT, K6, RT) two times, K2, K1 TBL, P3, Sl1, P11, Sl1, P5, Sl1, P11, Sl1, P3, K1 TBL, (K2, LT, K6, RT) two times, K2, Sl1, P1.

Rnd 73: With CC, K1 TBL, P3, Sl1, P6, Sl1, P4, Sl1, P6, Sl1, P3, Sl1, K3, 1/2 LC, K9, 1/2 LC, K1, 1/2 RC, K9, 1/2 RC, K3, Sl1, P3, Sl1, P6, Sl1, P4, Sl1, P6, Sl1, P3, K1 TBL, K1.

Rnd 74: With MC, Sl1, K3, LT, K4, RT, K4, LT, K4, RT, K3, K1 TBL, P5, Sl1, P11, Sl1, P1, Sl1, P11, Sl1, P5, K1 TBL, K3, LT, K4, RT, K4, LT, K4, RT, K3, Sl1, P1.

Rnd 75: With CC, K1 TBL, (P4, Sl1) two times, P6, (Sl1, P4) two times, Sl1, K5, 1/2 LC, K9, 1/1/1 LC, K9, 1/2 RC, K5, Sl1, (P4, Sl1) two times, P6, (Sl1, P4) two times, K1 TBL, K1.

Rnd 76: With MC, Sl1, K4, LT, K2, RT, K6, LT, K2, RT, K4, K1 TBL, P7, Sl1, P9, Sl1, P1, Sl1, P9, Sl1, P7, K1 TBL, K4, LT, K2, RT, K6, LT, K2, RT, K4, Sl1, P1.

Rnd 77: With CC, K1 TBL, P5, Sl1, P2, Sl1, P8, Sl1, P2, Sl1, P5, Sl1, K7, 1/2 LC, K5, 1/2 RC, K1, 1/2 LC, K5, 1/2 RC, K7, Sl1, P5, Sl1, P2, Sl1, P8, Sl1, P2, Sl1, P5, K1 TBL, K1.

Rnd 78: With MC, K5, LT, RT, K8, LT, RT, K5, K1 TBL, P9, (Sl1, P5) three times, Sl1, P9, K1 TBL, K5, LT, RT, K8, LT, RT, K5, Sl1, P1.

Rnd 79: With CC, K1 TBL, P6, Sl2, P10, Sl2, P6, Sl1, K9, 1/2 LC, K1, 1/2 RC, K5, 1/2 LC, K1, 1/2 RC, K9, Sl1, P6, Sl2, P10, Sl2, P6, K1 TBL, K1.

Rnd 80: With MC, K6, LT, K10, LT, K6, K1 TBL, P11, Sl1, P1, Sl1, P9, Sl1, P1, Sl1, P11, K1 TBL, K6, LT, K10, LT, K6, Sl1, P1.

Rnd 81: With CC, K1 TBL, P6, Sl2, P10, Sl2, P6, Sl1, K11, 1/1/1 RC, K9, 1/1/1 RC, K11, Sl1, P6, Sl2, P10, Sl2, P6, K1 TBL, K1.

Rnd 82: With MC, K5, RT, LT, K8, RT, LT, K5, K1 TBL, P11, Sl1, P1, Sl1, P9, Sl1, P1, Sl1, P11, K1 TBL, K5, RT, LT, K8, RT, LT, K5, Sl1, P1.

Rnd 83: With CC, K1 TBL, P5, Sl1, P2, Sl1, P8, Sl1, P2, Sl1, P5, Sl1, K9, 1/2 RC, K1, 1/2 LC, K5, 1/2 RC, K1, 1/2 LC, K9, Sl1, P5, Sl1, P2, Sl1, P8, Sl1, P2, Sl1, P5, K1 TBL, K1.

Rnd 84: With MC, K4, RT, K2, LT, K6, RT, K2, LT, K4, K1 TBL, P9, (Sl1, P5) three times, Sl1, P9, K1 TBL, K4, RT, K2, LT, K6, RT, K2, LT, K4, Sl1, P1.

Rnd 85: With CC, K1 TBL, (P4, Sl1) two times, P6, (Sl1, P4) two times, Sl1, K7, 1/2 RC, K5, 1/2 LC, K1, 1/2 RC, K5, 1/2 LC, K7, (Sl1, P4) two times, Sl1, P6, (Sl1, P4) two times, K1 TBL, K1.

Rnd 86: With MC, K3, RT, K4, LT, K4, RT, K,4, LT, K3, K1 TBL, P7, Sl1, P9, Sl1, P1, Sl1, P9, Sl1, P7, K1 TBL, K3, RT, K4, LT, K4, RT, K4, LT, K3, Sl1, P1.

Rnd 87: With CC, K1 TBL, P3, Sl1, P6, Sl1, P4, Sl1, P6, Sl1, P3, Sl1, K5, 1/2 RC, K9, 1/1/1 LC, K9, 1/2 LC, K5, Sl1, P3, Sl1, P6, Sl1, P4, Sl1, P6, Sl1, P3, K1 TBL, K1.

Rnd 88: With MC, K2, (RT, K6, LT, K2) two times, K1 TBL, P5, (Sl1, P1, Sl1, P9) two times, Sl1, P1, Sl1, P5, K1 TBL, (K2, RT, K6, LT) two times, K2, Sl1, P1.

Rnd 89: With CC, K1 TBL, (P2, Sl1, P8, Sl1) two times, P2, Sl1, K37, (Sl1, P2, Sl1, P8) two times, Sl1, P2, K1 TBL, K1.

DIRECTIONS

Body
With MC and using a Cable Cast On, CO 330 sts. Join in the rnd, being careful not to twist sts.

Rnd 1: Work Cable Pattern Rnd 1 over 94 sts, work Two-Color Garter Pattern to end.

Work as established through Rnd 89 of Cable Pattern.

BO all sts with MC.

Finishing
Weave in ends and block.

LEGEND

☐	**Main Color**
▦	**Contrasting Color**
☐	**Knit Stitch**
⊡	**Purl Stitch**
V	**Sl** Slip stitch purl-wise, with yarn in back
B	**K TBL** Knit stitch through the back loop
▱	**Right Twist (RT)** Sl1 to CN, hold in back; K1, K1 from CN
▱	**Left Twist (LT)** Sl1 to CN, hold in front; K1, K1 from CN
▱	**Cable 1 Over 2 Right (1/2 RC)** Sl2 to CN, hold in back; K1, K2 from CN
▱	**Cable 1 Over 2 Left (1/2 LC)** Sl1 to CN, hold in front; K2, K1 from CN
▱	**Cable 1 Over 1 Right, with center stitch (1/1/1 RC)** Sl2 to CN, hold in back; K1, Sl center st from CN back to left-hand needle and knit it; K1 from CN
▱	**Cable 1 Over 1 Left, with center stitch (1/1/1 LC)** Sl2 to CN, hold in front; K1, Sl center st from CN back to left-hand needle and knit it; K1 from CN
☐	**Pattern Repeat** Repeat these stitches once more at solid red gap

Cable Pattern

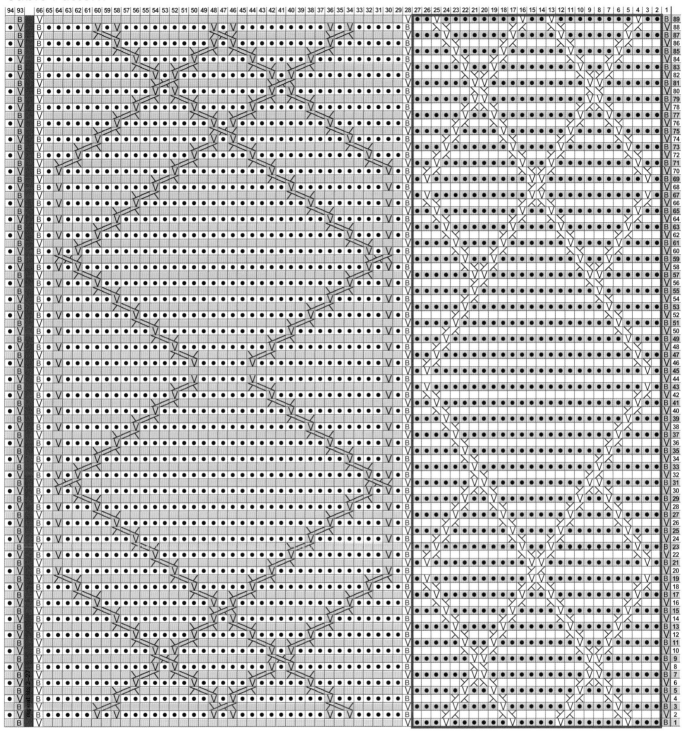

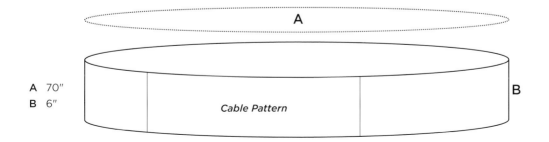

A 70"
B 6"

Cable Pattern

STANWOOD

by Allison Griffith

FINISHED MEASUREMENTS

Approximately 8.5″ depth, not including
points × 68.5″ width along outside curve

YARN

Hawthorne™ (fingering weight, 80%
Fine Superwash Highland Wool, 20%
Polyamide (Nylon); 357 yards/100g):
MC Slate Kettle 26688, C1 Macadam
Multi 27835, C2 Jade District Multi
27843, 1 hank each

NEEDLES

US 5 (3.75mm) 32″ or longer circular
needles, or size to obtain gauge

NOTIONS

Yarn Needle
Stitch Markers

GAUGE

21 sts and 42 rows = 4″ in Garter Stitch,
blocked (gauge is not crucial, but it will
affect finished size and yardage
requirements)

For pattern support, contact knittingontheneedles@gmail.com

Stanwood

Notes:

Stanwood is the best of both worlds: it's more practical than a shawl and more fun than a scarf. A great everyday accessory—with its garter squish and slight curve, it is perfect for throwing around your shoulders on cool autumn mornings as you head out the door.

Stanwood is a long, slightly curved shawlette, worked flat from the long end. The piece is knit in Garter Stitch, with contrasting stripes along the outer curve. Garter Stitch points along the outside of the shawl are worked using short rows.

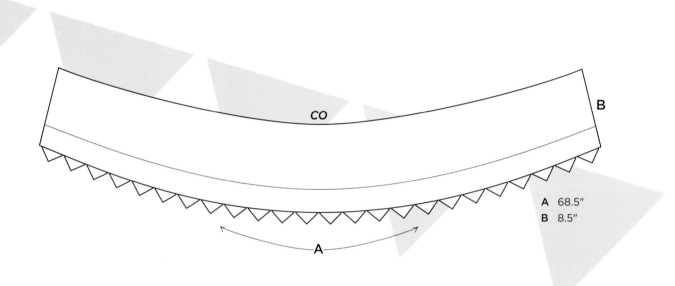

A 68.5"
B 8.5"

DIRECTIONS

With MC, loosely CO 288 sts.

Setup Row (WS): (K12, PM) to 12 sts before end, K12.
Knit 21 rows.

Inc Row (WS): (K6, M1R, K6, SM) to 12 sts before end, K6, M1R, K6. 312 sts.
Knit 23 rows.

Inc Row (WS): (K7, M1R, K6, SM) to 12 sts before end, K7, M1R, K6. 336 sts.
Knit eight rows. Break MC.

Stripes

Join and drop C1 and C2 as stated. Do not break yarn between stripes.

Rows 1–2: With C1, K across.
Rows 3–6: With C2, K across.
Rows 7–8: With C1, K across.
Rows 9: With C2, K across.
Rows 10 (WS Inc Row): With C2, (K7, M1R, K7, SM) to 12 sts before end, K7, M1R, K7. 360 sts.
Rows 11–12: With C2, K across.
Rows 13–14: With C1, K across.
Rep Rows 11–14 five more times.
Break C2. Cont working with C1.

Points

Points are worked using short rows.

Short Row 1 (RS): K1, W&T.
Short Row 2 and all other WS rows: K to end.
Short Row 3: K2, W&T.
Short Row 5: K3, W&T.
Short Row 7: K4, W&T.
Short Row 9: K5, W&T.
Short Row 11: K6, W&T.
Short Row 13: K7, W&T.
Short Row 15: K8, W&T.
Short Row 17: K9, W&T.
Short Row 19: K10, W&T.
Short Row 21: K11, W&T.
Short Row 23: K12, W&T.
Short Row 25: K13, W&T.
Short Row 27: K14, W&T.
Short Row 29: BO 15 sts, removing M as you come to it, W&T.
Rep Short Rows 2–29 23 more times. On the last repeat of Short Row 29, BO all sts.

Finishing

Weave in ends, wash, and block lightly.

SUNBOW

by Katy Banks

FINISHED MEASUREMENTS

85″ width × 21″ depth from top edge to border at deepest point

YARN

Stroll™ (fingering weight, 75% Superwash Merino Wool 25% Nylon; 231 yards/50g): MC White 26082, 4 balls

and

Stroll™ Tonal Mini Pack (fingering weight, 75% Fine Superwash Merino Wool, 25% Nylon; 462 yards/100g): C1–5 Radiant Reds 44541, 1 pack

NEEDLES

US 6 (4 mm) 60″ or longer circular needles, or size to obtain gauge

US 8 (5mm) DPNs or straight or circular needles, or two sizes larger than size used to obtain gauge (for bind off)

NOTIONS

Yarn Needle

Blocking Pins and/or Wires

GAUGE

20 sts and 28 rows = 4″ in Stockinette Stitch on smaller needles, blocked (gauge is not crucial, but it will affect finished size and yardage requirements)

For pattern support, contact katybanksdesigns@gmail.com

Sunbow

Notes:

Created when sunlight is refracted by a fine mist or spray, the sunbow is sometimes rather modest compared to its grandiose cousin, the rainbow. Demure hints of color tiptoe their way across this shawl, only revealing their true glory when they sweep together across the border edge.

The Sunbow shawl is an asymmetrical crescent shawl worked from the top down. Wedges of Stockinette Stitch shaped with short rows fill the spaces between slip stitch arcs of color. The colors are then worked in reverse order to create the Garter Stitch border.

P-YO-P

Into 1 st: purl, then yarn over, then purl, to inc from 1 to 3 sts.

K-YO-K

Into 1 st: knit, then yarn over, then knit, to inc from 1 to 3 sts.

DIRECTIONS

Garter Tab Setup

With MC and smaller needles, using Judy's Magic Cast On, CO 3 sts on each needle.

Knit four rows (2 ridges).

After last row, do not turn work; YO, rotate work 90 degrees, PU and K 1 in valley between ridges, YO, rotate work 90 degrees, K3 from CO edge. 9 sts.

Next Row (WS): K3, P-YO-P, P1, P-YO-P, K3. 4 sts inc; 13 sts.

Crescent Base

Row 1 (RS): Cont with MC, K3, YO, K to last 3 sts, YO, K3. 2 sts inc.

Row 2 (WS): K3, P-YO-P, P to last 4 sts, P-YO-P, K3. 4 sts inc.
Rep Rows 1–2 nineteen more times. 133 sts.

Slip Stitch Stripes & Short Rows Wedges

This section is worked four times; numbers that change in subsequent repeats are presented in [brackets] representing the first through fourth time this section is worked.

Row 1 (RS): Cont with MC, K3, YO, K to last 3 sts, YO, K3. 2 sts inc.

Row 2 (WS): K3, K-YO-K, K to last 4 sts, K-YO-K, K3. 4 sts inc.

Row 3: Join C1 [C2, C3, C4], K3, (Sl1 WYIB, K1) to last 2 [3, 2, 3] sts, K to end.

Row 4: K3 [4, 3, 4], (Sl1 WYIF, K1) to last 2 sts, K2. Break C1 [C2, C3, C4].

Row 5: With MC, K3, YO, K to last 3 sts, YO, K3. 2 sts inc.

Row 6: K3, K-YO-K, K to last 4 sts, K-YO-K, K3. 4 sts inc.

Row 7: K3, YO, K5 [6, 7, 8], W&T. 1 st inc.

Row 8: P to last 4 sts, P-YO-P, K3. 2 sts inc.

Row 9: K3, YO, K to 7 [12, 17, 22] sts past wrapped st (working wrap tog with wrapped st), W&T. 1 st inc.

Row 10: P to last 4 sts, P-YO-P, K3. 2 sts inc.
Rep Rows 9–10 15 more times.

Row 11: K3, YO, K to last 3 sts, YO, K3. 2 sts inc.

Row 12: K3, P-YO-P, P to last 4 sts, P-YO-P, K3. 4 sts inc.
Rep Rows 11–12 two more times. 214 [295, 376, 457] sts.
Rep this section from Row 1 until you have four Slip Stitch Stripes alternating with four Short Rows Wedges.

Fifth Slip Stitch Stripe

Cont with MC.

Row 1: K3, YO, K to last 3 sts, YO, K3. 459 sts.

Row 2: K3, K-YO-K, K to last 4 sts, K-YO-K, K3. 463 sts.

Row 3: Join C5, K3, (Sl1 WYIB, K1) to last 2 sts, K2.

Row 4: K3, (Sl1 WYIF, K1) to last 2 sts, K2.
Break C5.

Garter Stripes Border

Cont with MC.

Row 1: K3, YO, K to last 3 sts, YO, K3. 2 sts inc.

Row 2: K3, K-YO-K, K to last 4 sts, K-YO-K, K3. 4 sts inc.
Rep Rows 1–2 two more times. Break MC. 481 sts.
Rep this section with C5 (499 sts), then with C4 (517 sts), then with C3 (535 sts), then with C2 (553 sts).
Join C1 and knit five rows.

BO: With larger needles, K1, (Sl the newly knit st to LH needle, K2tog) to end, and fasten off.

Finishing

Weave in all ends. Wash and block.

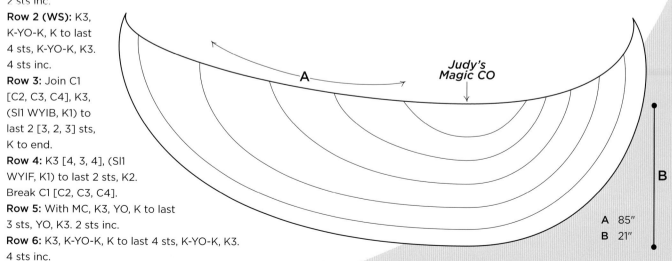

A   85"
B   21"

SUNDAY VIBES

by Emily O'Brien

FINISHED MEASUREMENTS

68.25" width × 16.75" depth

YARN

Hawthorne™ (fingering weight, 80%
Fine Superwash Highland Wool, 20%
Polyamide (Nylon); 357 yards/100g):
C1 Ashland Tonal 27410, C2 Corvallis
Tonal 27401, C3 Hayden Multi 27840,
1 hank each

NEEDLES

US 4 (3.5mm) 40–47" circular needles,
or size to obtain gauge

NOTIONS

Yarn Needle
Stitch Markers
Blocking Pins and/or Wires
Cardboard Piece (2" wide, for mini
tassels)

GAUGE

25 sts and 50 rows = 4" in Garter Stitch,
blocked (gauge is not crucial, but it will
affect finished size and yardage
requirements)

Sunday Vibes

Notes:

The perfect project to knit while chilling in bed with some coffee on a lazy Sunday morning is also the absolute best shawl to wear on an afternoon jaunt to the farmer's market.

Sunday Vibes is a crescent shawl worked flat that grows by two stitches on the ends of every row. It features easy Garter Stitch sections with eyelets and color changes to keep it interesting. The chevron finale adds a graphic pop to the shawl. Adorable mini tassels complete the look.

Carry the color not being worked up the side. Only break yarn when indicated in pattern for fewer ends to weave in.

Chevrons pattern is both written and charted. Chart is worked flat; read RS rows (odd numbers) from right to left, and WS rows (even numbers) from left to right.

KFBF (knit front, back, front)
Knit into the front, then back, then front of stitch. 2 sts inc.

Chevrons (worked flat)

Row 1 (RS): With C2, K3, SM, KFB, K to 1 st before M, KFB, SM, K3. 2 sts inc.

Row 2 (WS): With C2, Rep Row 1.

Row 3: With C2, K3, SM, KFB, P to 1 st before M, KFB, SM, K3. 2 sts inc.

Row 4: With C2, Rep Row 1.

Row 5: With C3, K3, SM, KFB, *K2tog, K3, (K1, P1, K1) in 1 st, K3, SSK; rep from * to 1 st before M, KFB, SM, K3. 2 sts inc.

Row 6: With C3, K3, SM, KFB, P to 1 st before M, KFB, SM, K3. 2 sts inc.

Row 7: With C3, K3, SM, KFB, K2, *K2tog, K3, (K1, P1, K1) in 1 st, K3, SSK; rep from * to 3 sts before M, K2, KFB, SM, K3. 2 sts inc.

Row 8: With C3, Rep Row 6.

Row 9: With C3, K3, SM, KFB, K4, *K2tog, K3, (K1, P1, K1) in 1 st, K3, SSK; rep from * to 5 sts before M, K4, KFB, SM, K3. 2 sts inc.

Row 10: With C3, K3, SM, KFBF, P to 1 st before M, KFBF, SM, K3. 4 sts inc.

Rep Rows 1–10 for pattern.

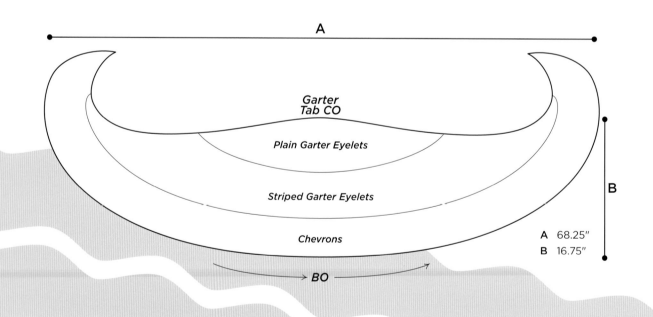

DIRECTIONS

Garter Tab Cast On
Loosely CO 3 sts using C1.
Knit eight rows.
Setup Row 1 (RS): K3, do not turn, PM, PU and K 4 sts from Garter edge, PM, PU and K 3 sts from CO edge. 10 sts.
Setup Row 2 (WS): K3, SM, KFB, K2, KFB, SM, K3. 12 sts.

Plain Garter Eyelets
Row 1 (RS): K3, SM, KFB, K to 1 st before M, KFB, SM, K3. 2 sts inc.
Rows 2–16: Rep Row 1.
Row 17: K3, SM, KFB, (YO, K2tog) to 1 st before M, KFB, SM, K3. 2 sts inc.
Row 18: Rep Row 1.
Rep Rows 1–18 three more times. 156 sts.
Rep Rows 1–16 once more. 188 sts.

Striped Garter Eyelets
Row 1 (RS): With C2, K3, SM, KFB, K to 1 st before M, KFB, SM, K3. 2 sts inc.
Row 2 (WS): With C2, Rep Row 1.
Row 3: With C1, K3, SM, KFB, K to 1 st before M, KFB, SM, K3. 2 sts inc.
Row 4: With C1, Rep Row 3.
Rows 5–16: Rep Rows 1–4.
Row 17: With C2, K3, SM, KFB, (YO, K2tog) to 1 st before M, KFB, SM, K3. 2 sts inc.
Row 18: With C2, Rep Row 1.
Row 19: With C1, Rep Row 3.
Row 20: With C1, Rep Row 3.
Rep Rows 1–20 two more times. 308 sts.
Break C1.

Chevrons
Work Chevrons pattern from chart or written instructions five times. 418 sts.
Break C3.

Garter Border
Row 1 (RS): With C2, K3, SM, KFB, K to 1 st before M, KFB, SM, K3. 2 sts inc.
Rep Row 1 three more times. 426 sts.
Loosely BO all sts.

Finishing
Weave in ends, wash, and block to diagram. Use a pin at each point of the chevrons so the Garter Border has points.

Mini Tassels
Use a 2″ wide piece of cardboard as a template. Wrap C1 around template twelve times. Cut yarn. Cut a 10″ piece of yarn, tie end of tassel that is all folds (not cut ends), leave ends to attach to shawl. Slide bundle off cardboard. Cut 8″ piece of yarn, use to wrap around approx 0.5″ away from tie, wrap 3–4 times. Tie a knot, wrap again, tie another knot. Snip loops on other end of bundle. Trim ends to be even. Make 36 tassels.
Attach one tassel to each of the chevron points.

Chevrons

LEGEND

▨	**Color 2**
☐	**Color 3**
▰	**No Stitch** Placeholder—no stitch made
☐	**K** RS: Knit stitch WS: Purl stitch
•	**P** RS: Purl stitch WS: Knit stitch
╱	**K2tog** Knit 2 stitches together as one stitch
╲	**SSK** Slip, slip, knit slipped stitches together
Ⲅ	**KFB** Knit into the front and back of the stitch
þ	**KFB on WS** WS: Knit into the front and back of stitch
ⲫ	**KFBF on WS** WS: Knit into the front, then back, then front of stitch
Ⅴ	**KPK** Knit 1, then Purl 1, then Knit 1 into the same stitch
☐	**Pattern Repeat**
∣	**Slip Marker**

WAKEROBIN

by M K Nance

FINISHED MEASUREMENTS

60″ outer wingspan × 8.5″ depth

YARN

Capretta™ Superwash (fingering weight, 80% Fine Superwash Merino Wool, 10% Cashmere, 10% Nylon; 230 yards/50g): MC Moonstone 2643, CC Meridian 27637, 1 ball each

NEEDLES

US 4 (3.5mm) 24–32″ circular needles, or size to obtain gauge

NOTIONS

Yarn Needle
Stitch Markers
Cable Needle

GAUGE

24 sts and 40 rows = 4″ in Garter Stitch, blocked

For pattern support, contact mknanceknit@gmail.com

Wakerobin

Notes:

This shawlette is made for a walk in the woods searching for wakerobins (also known as trillium) on a damp Oregon spring morning.

This is a round shawl or shawlette designed for a wool-based fingering weight yarn. It plays with slipped stitches and cables floating over Garter Stitch. Break yarn that is not in use for more than four rows.

Stitch Pattern is both written and charted. Chart is worked flat; read RS rows (odd numbers) from right to left, and WS rows (even numbers) from left to right.

Stitch Pattern (worked flat)

Row 1 (RS): With CC, K across.

Row 2 (WS): With CC, K across.

Row 3: With CC, K3, (K1, M1, K14, M1) ten times, K4. 177 sts.

Row 4: With CC, K4, (K1, [P2, K4] two times, P2, K2) ten times, K3.

Row 5: With CC, K3, (K1, M1, K16, M1) ten times, K4. 197 sts.

Row 6: With CC, K4, (K2, [P2, K4] two times, P2, K3) ten times, K3.

Row 7: With CC, K3, (K1, M1, [1/2 RC, 1/2 LC] three times, M1) ten times, K4. 217 sts.

Row 8: With CC, K4, (K1, P1, [K4, P2] two times, K4, P1, K2) ten times, K3.

Row 9: With MC, K3, (K1, M1, K1, Sl1, [K4, Sl2] two times, K4, Sl1, K1, M1) ten times, K4. 237 sts.

Row 10: With MC, K4, (K2, Sl1 WYIF, [K4, Sl2 WYIF] two times, K4, Sl1 WYIF, K3) ten times, K3.

Row 11: With CC, K3, (K3, [1/2 LC, 1/2 RC] three times, K2) ten times, K4.

Row 12: With CC, K4, ([K4, P2] three times, K5) ten times, K3.

Row 13: With MC, K3, (K1, M1, [K4, Sl2] three times, K4, M1) ten times, K4. 257 sts.

Row 14: With MC, K4, (K5, [Sl2 WYIF, K4] two times, Sl2 WYIF, K6) ten times, K3.

Row 15: With CC, K3, (K4, [1/2 RC, 1/2 LC] three times, K3) ten times, K4.

Row 16: With CC, K4, (K3, P1, [K4, P2] two times, K4, P1, K4) ten times, K3.

Row 17: With MC, K3, (K1, M1, K3, Sl1, [K4, Sl2] two times, K4, Sl1, K3, M1) ten times, K4. 277 sts.

Row 18: With MC, K4, (K4, Sl1 WYIF, [K4, Sl2 WYIF] two times, K4, Sl1 WYIF, K5) ten times, K3.

Row 19: With CC, K3, (K5, [1/2 LC, 1/2 RC] three times, K4) ten times, K4.

Row 20: With CC, K4, (K6, [P2, K4] two times, P2, K7) ten times, K3.

Row 21: With MC, K3, (K1, M1, K6, [Sl2, K4] two times, Sl2, K6, M1) ten times, K4. 297 sts.

Row 22: With MC, K4, (K7, [Sl2 WYIF, K4] two times, Sl2 WYIF, K8) ten times, K3.

Rows 23–24: With CC, K across.

Row 25: With MC, K3, (K1, M1, K28, M1) ten times, K4. 317 sts.

Row 26: With MC, K across.

Rows 27–28: With CC, K across.

Row 29: With MC, K3, (K1, M1, K30, M1) ten times, K4. 337 sts.

Row 30: With MC, K across.

Rows 31–32: With CC, K across.

Rows 33–34: With MC, K across.

Row 35: With MC, K3, (K1, M1, K32, M1) ten times, K4. 357 sts.

Rows 36–37: With MC, K across.

Row 38: With MC, K4, ([K4, P2] five times, K5) ten times, K3.

Rows 39–40: Rep Rows 37–38.

Row 41: With MC, K3, (K3, [1/2 RC, 1/2 LC] five times, K2) ten times, K4.

Row 42: With MC, K4, (K2, P1, [K4, P2] four times, K4, P1, K3) ten times, K3.

Row 43: With CC, K3, (K1, M1, K2, Sl1, [K4, Sl2] four times, K4, Sl1, K2, M1) ten times, K4. 377 sts.

Row 44: With CC, K4, (K3, Sl1 WYIF, [K4, Sl2 WYIF] four times, K4, Sl1 WYIF, K4) ten times, K3.

Row 45: With MC, K3, (K4, [1/2 LC, 1/2 RC] five times, K3) ten times, K4.

Row 46: With MC, K4, (K5, [P2, K4] four times, P2, K6) ten times, K3.

Row 47: With CC, K3, (K6, [Sl2, K4] four times, Sl2, K5) ten times, K4.

Row 48: With CC, K4, (K5, [Sl2 WYIF, K4] four times, Sl2 WYIF, K6) ten times, K3.

Row 49: With MC, K3, (K4, [1/2 RC, 1/2 LC] five times, K3) ten times, K4.

Row 50: With MC, K4, (K3, P1, [K4, P2] four times, K4, P1, K4) ten times, K3.

Row 51: With CC, K3, (K1, M1, K3, Sl1, [K4, Sl2] four times, K4, Sl1, K3, M1) ten times, K4. 397 sts.

Row 52: With CC, K4, (K4, Sl1 WYIF, [K4, Sl2 WYIF] four times, K4, Sl1 WYIF, K5) ten times, K3.

Row 53: With MC, K3, (K5, [1/2 LC, 1/2 RC] five times, K4) ten times, K4.

Row 54: With MC, K4, (K6, [P2, K4] four times, P2, K7) ten times, K3.

Row 55: With CC, K3, (K7, [Sl2, K4] four times, Sl2, K6) ten times, K4.

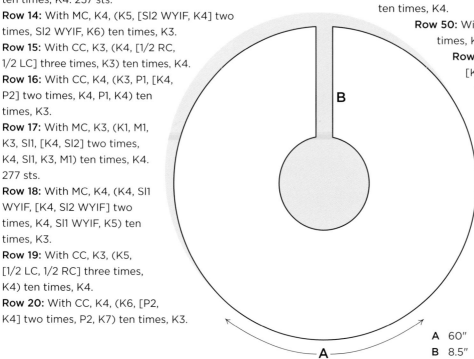

A 60"
B 8.5"

Row 56: With CC, K4, (K6, (Sl2 WYIF, K4) four times, Sl2 WYIF, K7) ten times, K3.

Row 57: With MC, K3, (K5, [1/2 RC, 1/2 LC] five times, K4) ten times, K4.

Row 58: With MC, K4, (K4, P1, [K4, P2] five times, K4) ten times, K3.

Row 59: With CC, K3, (K1, M1, K4, Sl1, [K4, Sl2] four times, K4, Sl1, K4, M1) ten times, K4. 417 sts.

Row 60: With CC, K4, (K5, Sl1 WYIF, [K4, Sl2 WYIF] four times, K4, Sl1 WYIF, K6) ten times, K3.

Row 61: With MC, K3, (K6, [1/2 LC, 1/2 RC] five times, K5) ten times, K4.

Row 62: With MC, K4, (K7, [P2, K4] four times, P2, K8) ten times, K3.

Rows 63–64: With CC, K across.

Rows 65–66: With MC, K across.

Rows 67–68: With CC, K across.

Rows 69–72: With MC, K across.

Rows 73–74: With CC, K across.

DIRECTIONS

Loosely CO 157 sts.

Setup Row (WS): With CC, K across.

Work Stitch Pattern Rows 1–74 from chart or written instructions. 417 sts.

Rep Rows 63–74 once more.

Optional: Rep these rows more times to extend height of piece, ending with a WS row.

BO all sts in pattern.

Finishing

Weave in ends, wash, and block to diagram.

Stitch Pattern

LEGEND

<table>
<tr><td>☐</td><td>Main Color</td></tr>
</table>

☐ **Main Color**

☐ **Contrasting Color**

⬛ **No Stitch**
Placeholder—no stitch made

K
☐ RS: Knit stitch
WS: Purl stitch

P
● RS: Purl stitch
WS: Knit stitch

Sl
V RS: Slip stitch purl-wise, with yarn in back
WS: Slip stitch purl-wise, with yarn in front

M1
M Make 1 stitch

Cable 1 Over 2 Right (1/2 RC)
Sl2 to CN, hold in back; K1, K2 from CN

Cable 1 Over 2 Left (1/2 LC)
Sl1 to CN, hold in front; K2, K1 from CN

☐ **Stitch Pattern Repeat**

☐ **Horizontal Pattern Repeat**

Glossary

Common Stitches & Techniques

Slipped Stitches (Sl)
Always slip stitches purl-wise with yarn held to the wrong side of work, unless noted otherwise in the pattern.

Make 1 Left-Leaning Stitch (M1L)
Inserting LH needle from front to back, PU the horizontal strand between the st just worked and the next st, and K TBL.

Make 1 Right-Leaning Stitch (M1R)
Inserting LH needle from back to front, PU the horizontal strand between the st just worked and the next st, and K TFL.

Slip, Slip, Knit (SSK)
(Sl1 K-wise) twice; insert LH needle into front of these 2 sts and knit them together.

Centered Double Decrease (CDD)
Slip first and second sts together as if to work K2tog; K1; pass 2 slipped sts over the knit st.

Stockinette Stitch (St st, flat over any number of sts)
Row 1 (RS): Knit all sts.
Row 2 (WS): Purl all sts.
Rep Rows 1-2 for pattern.
St st in the round: Knit every rnd.

Garter Stitch (in the round over any number of sts)
Rnd 1: Purl all sts.
Rnd 2: Knit all sts.
Rep Rnds 1-2 for pattern.
Garter Stitch flat: Knit every row.
(One Garter ridge is comprised of two rows/rnds.)

1x1 Rib (flat or in the round, over an even number of sts)
Row/Rnd 1: (K1, P1) to end of row/rnd.
Rep Row/Rnd 1 for pattern.

2x2 Rib (flat over a multiple of 4 sts plus 2)
Row 1 (RS): K2, (P2, K2) to end of row.
Row 2 (WS): P2, (K2, P2) to end of row.
Rep Rows 1-2 for pattern.

2x2 Rib (in the round over a multiple of 4 sts)
Rnd 1: (K2, P2) to end of rnd.
Rep Rnd 1 for pattern.

Magic Loop Technique
A technique using one long circular needle to knit in the round around a small circumference. A tutorial can be found at tutorials.knitpicks.com/wptutorials/magic-loop.

Knitting in the Round with Two Circular Needles
A technique using two long circulars to knit around a small circumference. A tutorial can be found at tutorials.knitpicks.com/knitting-in-the-round-with-2-circular-needles.

Backward Loop Cast On
A simple, all-purpose cast on that can be worked mid-row. Also called Loop, Single, or E-Wrap Cast On. A tutorial can be found at tutorials.knitpicks.com/loop-cast-on.

Long Tail Cast On
Fast and neat once you get the hang of it. Also referred to as the Slingshot Cast On. A tutorial can be found at tutorials.knitpicks.com/long-tail-cast-on.

Cabled Cast On
A strong and nice looking basic cast on that can be worked mid-project. A tutorial can be found at tutorials.knitpicks.com/cabled-cast-on.

3-Needle Bind Off
Used to easily seam two rows of live stitches together. A tutorial can be found at tutorials.knitpicks.com/3-needle-bind-off.

Abbreviations

approx	approximately	KFB	knit into front and back of stitch
BO	bind off		
BOR	beginning of round	K-wise	knit-wise
CN	cable needle	LH	left hand
C (1, 2...)	color (1, 2...)	M	marker
CC	contrast color	M1	make 1 stitch
CDD	centered double decrease (*see above*)	M1L	make 1 left-leaning stitch (*see above*)
		M1R	make 1 right-leaning stitch (*see above*)
CO	cast on		
cont	continue		
dec(s)	decrease(es)	MC	main color
DPN(s)	double pointed needle(s)	P	purl
		P2tog	purl 2 stitches together
inc(s)	increase(s)	P3tog	purl 3 stitches together
K	knit		
K2tog	knit 2 stitches together	PM	place marker
		PFB	purl into front and back of stitch
K3tog	knit 3 stitches together		

PSSO	pass slipped stitch over	SSP	slip, slip, purl these 2 stitches together through back loop
PU	pick up		
P-wise	purl-wise	SSSK	slip, slip, slip, knit these 3 stitches together (like SSK)
rep	repeat		
Rev St st	reverse stockinette stitch		
RH	right hand	St st	stockinette stitch (*see above*)
rnd(s)	round(s)		
RS	right side	st(s)	stitch(es)
Sk	skip	TBL	through back loop
SK2P	slip 1, knit 2 together, pass slipped stitch over	TFL	through front loop
		tog	together
SKP	slip, knit, pass slipped stitch over	W&T	wrap & turn (for short rows; *see next pg*)
Sl	slip (*see above*)		
SM	slip marker	WE	work even
SSK	slip, slip, knit these 2 stitches together (*see above*)	WS	wrong side
		WYIB	with yarn in back
		WYIF	with yarn in front
		YO	yarn over

Cables (Including without a Cable Needle)

Tutorials for 1 over 1 cables can be found at blog.knitpicks.com/tutorial-1-over-1-cables-without-a-cable-needle. Tutorials for standard cables can be found at blog.knitpicks.com/tutorial-introduction-to-cables.

Felted Join (to splice yarn)

One method for joining a new length of yarn to the end of one that is already being used. A tutorial can be found at tutorials.knitpicks.com/felted-join.

Mattress Stitch

A neat, invisible seaming method that uses the bars between the first and second stitches on the edges. A tutorial can be found at tutorials.knitpicks.com/mattress-stitch.

Provisional Cast On (crochet method)

Used to cast on stitches that are also a row of live stitches, so they can be put onto a needle and used later.

Directions: Using a crochet hook, make a slipknot, then hold knitting needle in left hand, hook in right. With yarn in back of needle, work a chain st by pulling yarn over needle and through chain st. Move yarn back to behind needle, and rep for the number of sts required. Chain a few more sts off the needle, then break yarn and pull end through last chain. (CO sts may be incorrectly mounted; if so, work into backs of these sts.) To unravel later (when sts need to be picked up), pull chain end out; chain should unravel, leaving live sts. A video tutorial can be found at tutorials.knitpicks.com/crocheted-provisional-cast-on.

Provisional Cast On (crochet chain method)

Same result as the crochet method above, but worked differently, so you may prefer one or the other.

Directions: With a crochet hook, use scrap yarn to make a slipknot and chain the number of sts to be cast on, plus a few extra sts. Insert tip of knitting needle into first bump of crochet chain. Wrap project yarn around needle as if to knit, and pull yarn through crochet chain, forming first st. Rep this process until you have cast on the correct number of sts. To unravel later (when sts need to be picked up), pull chain out, leaving live sts. A photo tutorial can be found at tutorials.knitpicks.com/crocheted-provisional-cast-on.

Judy's Magic Cast On

This method creates stitches coming out in opposite directions from a seamless center line, perfect for starting toe-up socks.

Directions: Make a slipknot and place loop around one of the two needles; anchor loop counts as first st. Hold needles tog, with needle that yarn is attached to on top. In other hand, hold yarn so tail goes over index finger and yarn attached to ball goes over thumb. Bring tip of bottom needle over strand of yarn on finger (top strand), around and under yarn and back up, making a loop around needle. Pull loop snug. Bring top needle (with slipknot) over yarn tail on thumb (bottom strand), around and under yarn and back up, making a loop around needle. Pull loop snug. Cont casting on sts until desired number is reached; top yarn strand always wraps around bottom needle, and bottom yarn strand always wraps around top needle. A tutorial can be found at tutorials.knitpicks.com/judys-magic-cast-on.

Stretchy Bind Off

Directions: K2, *insert LH needle into front of 2 sts on RH needle and knit them tog—1 st remains on RH needle. K1; rep from * until all sts have been bound off. A tutorial can be found at tutorials.knitpicks.com/go-your-own-way-socks-toe-up-part-7-binding-off.

Jeny's Surprisingly Stretchy Bind Off (for 1x1 Rib)

Directions: Reverse YO, K1, pass YO over; *YO, P1, pass YO and previous st over P1; reverse YO, K1, pass YO and previous st over K1; rep from * until 1 st is left, then break working yarn and pull it through final st to complete BO.

Kitchener Stitch (also called Grafting)

Seamlessly join two sets of live stitches together.

Directions: With an equal number of sts on two needles, break yarn leaving a tail approx four times as long as the row of sts, and thread through a blunt yarn needle. Hold needles parallel with WSs facing in and both needles pointing to the right. Perform Step 2 on the first front st, then Step 4 on the first back st, then continue from Step 1, always pulling yarn tightly so the grafted row tension matches the knitted fabric:

Step 1: Pull yarn needle K-wise through front st and drop st from knitting needle.

Step 2: Pull yarn needle P-wise through next front st, leaving st on knitting needle.

Step 3: Pull yarn needle P-wise through first back st and drop st from knitting needle.

Step 4: Pull yarn needle K-wise through next back st, leaving st on knitting needle.

Rep Steps 1-4 until all sts have been grafted together, finishing by working Step 1 through the last remaining front st, then Step 3 through the last remaining back st. Photo tutorials can be found at knitpicks.com/learning-center/learn-to-knit/kitchener.

Short Rows

There are several options for how to handle short rows, so you may see different suggestions/intructions in a pattern.

Wrap and Turn (W&T) (one option for Short Rows)

Work until the st to be wrapped. If knitting: Bring yarn to front, Sl next st P-wise, return yarn to back; turn work, and Sl wrapped st onto RH needle. Cont across row. If purling: Bring yarn to back of work, Sl next st P-wise, return yarn to front; turn work and Sl wrapped st onto RH needle. Cont across row.

Picking up Wraps: Work to wrapped st. If knitting: Insert RH needle under wrap, then through wrapped st K-wise; K st and wrap tog. If purling: Sl wrapped st P-wise onto RH needle, use LH needle to lift wrap and place it onto RH needle; Sl wrap and st back onto LH needle, and P tog.

A tutorial for W&T can be found at tutorials.knitpicks.com/short-rows-wrap-and-turn-or-wt.

German Short Rows (another option for Short Rows)

Work to turning point; turn. WYIF, Sl first st P-wise. Bring yarn over back of right needle, pulling firmly to create a "double stitch" on RH needle. If next st is a K st, leave yarn at back; if next st is a P st, bring yarn to front between needles. When it's time to work into double st, knit both strands tog.

THIS COLLECTION FEATURES

Gloss™
Fingering Weight
70% Merino Wool, 30% Silk

Capretta™ Superwash
Fingering Weight
80% Fine Superwash Merino Wool,
10% Cashmere, 10% Nylon

Chroma™
Fingering Weight
70% Superwash Wool, 30% Nylon

Hawthorne™ Multi, Kettle, Tonal, Speckle
Fingering Weight
80% Fine Superwash Highland Wool,
20% Polyamide (Nylon)

Stroll™ Hand Painted, Tweed, Minis, Gradient
Fingering Weight
75% Fine Superwash Merino Wool,
25% Nylon

View these beautiful
yarns and more at
www.KnitPicks.com

Knit Picks®

Knit Picks yarn is both luxe and affordable—a seeming contradiction
trounced! But it's not just about the pretty colors; we also care
deeply about fiber quality and fair labor practices, leaving you with
a gorgeously reliable product you'll turn to time and time again.